CW00729663

30130 144602520

Shock Tactics

A Farce

John Dole

Samuel French – London
New York – Sydney – Toronto – Hollywood

ii

SHOCK TACTICS

This play was first produced at the Playhouse, Erith, on 24th November 1965, with the following cast:

MRS TRUDGE	*Eileen Hullett*
PETER PULLER	*Colin Bailey*
FRED	*Pat Dole*
AUNT ESTHER	*Betty Cottee*
MARY SHAW	*Margaret Robinson*
GEORGE SHAW	*Frank Poole*
MARJORIE SHAW	*Audrey Christianson*
ALBERT SHORTER	*Chris Crooks*
POPPY BLOSSOM	*Jeanne Millett*
UNCLE BEN	*Eric Cornish*
TAXIMAN	*Neil Jarman*

Directed by EVE PRESTAGE

The action takes place in the living-room of Mr. and Mrs. Shaw's house in England.

ACT ONE	An evening in May
ACT TWO	Next morning
ACT THREE	After lunch, the same day

No character in this play is intended to portray any specific person, alive or dead.

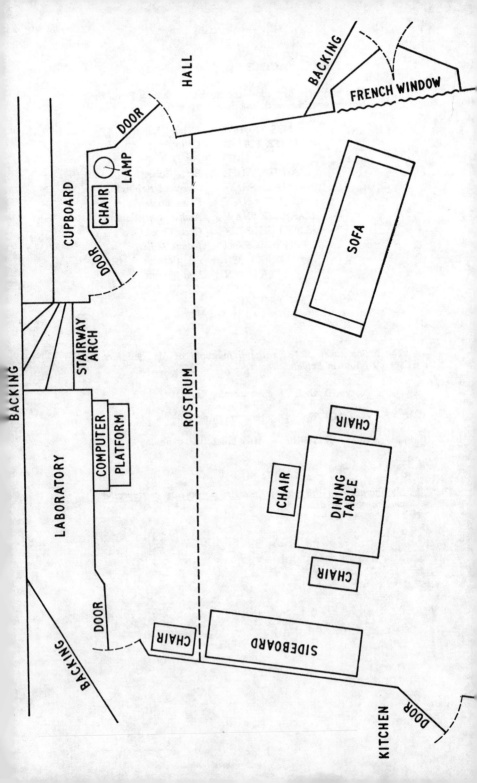

ACT I*

The action takes place in the living-room of the Shaws' house in a quiet corner of England.

It is a pleasant if rather untidy room. The furniture was originally good and solid and has clearly given years of excellent service and taken some hard knocks in the process. The décor is modern and striking, in particular the motif on one wall which incorporates a pattern of test-tubes, retorts and cog-wheels to suggest the 'Progress of Science.'

D.L. is a window alcove with floor-length curtains drawn across to conceal a french window. U.L. a door leads to the hall and front door. Just Left of C.B. the beginnings of a stair-case seen through archway and curving out of sight after the first few steps. L.B. and apparently under the stairs, a large cupboard door with a notice on it: 'Danger High Voltage.' U.R. another door marked 'Private' which leads to the laboratory. D.R. yet another door leading to the kitchen. The back third of the room is raised one step.

A sofa stands obliquely L.C. with brightly covered cushions, magazines and a library book. A standard lamp U.L. between the hall door and the cupboard. Next to it a dining chair. Against the wall R. a large side-board with various bric-à-brac including the innards of an old clock, a plaster bust which could be anyone from Galileo to Madame Curie, a telephone, a transistor radio, a bottle of scotch and a half-empty bottle of fruit-juice. R.C. a small dining table with three chairs. A fourth chair is tucked away above the sideboard. More magazines and a newspaper are strewn on the table and, in the centre, a vase of flowers. On the walls U.L. and U.R. two pleasant pictures of Spanish dancing girls and, less attractive, across the back wall festoons of wires leading from the door marked 'Private' to the cupboard.

Just R. of the staircase and apparently set in the wall is a most curious object. It looks rather like a cross between a weighing machine and a penny-in-the-slot fortune telling gadget from a fairground. It is complete with coloured dial and pointer and a row of knobs in selected

---

* Paragraph 3 on page ii of this Acting Edition regarding photocopying and video-recording should be carefully read.

*colours. In front of it is a small step and over the top, also set in the
wall, what appears to be the loud-speaker of a wireless set.*

*When the curtain rises the room is deserted. The main lights are on
and the curtains drawn across the alcove.*

> *A door-bell rings off L. and after a moment* MRS. TRUDGE
> *enters from the kitchen D.R. She is a rather faded lady
> of 50 or so who joined the household some years ago as
> a daily help and has since become a permanent affliction.
> She enjoys a bad leg and the miseries and is wearing an
> overall apron and an old blue hat heavily decorated with
> fruit. She is carrying a long pair of fire tongs.*
>
> *She mutters to herself as she limps across to the door
> U.L.*

MRS. TRUDGE Get finished some time, I suppose. Pity they can't answer
the door theirselves.

(The doorbell rings again.)

All right, all right. I'm coming. I 'aven't got roller
skates!

> *(She disappears through the door and we hear the mur-
> mur of voices in the hall. After a moment* PETER PULLER
> *appears, followed closely by* MRS. TRUDGE. *He is a
> reasonably presentable young fellow of about 25,
> decently if rather uncomfortably dressed in a dark suit
> and a tight white shirt. He looks round enquiringly.)*

(aggressively) Well, what do you want? I can't stand
about 'ere all day.

PETER I wanted to speak to Mr. Shaw actually.

MRS. TRUDGE 'Ere, you ain't one of them electrical fellows, are you?

PETER Er—no!

MRS. TRUDGE *(waving the tongs about)* Dear, oh dear! We 'ad enough
trouble with the last one 'oo came. 'E left a funny
smell under the stairs.

(She indicates the cupboard door U.L.)

PETER How unfortunate.

MRS. TRUDGE *(darkly)* Hozone 'e said it was. Smelled more like drains
to me.

PETER Quite. Well, I'll try not to leave any—er—traces. Mr.
Shaw?

MRS. TRUDGE 'E ain't in.

PETER   Oh!

MRS. TRUDGE 'E's out. Lecturing. And the missus is with 'im.

PETER   And Mary—er—Miss Shaw?

MRS. TRUDGE Oh, titivating in 'er room if I knows 'er.

PETER   Could I have a word with her, do you think? I'm Peter
             —Peter Puller.

MRS. TRUDGE Don't see why not. I'll give 'er a shout. (*She moves
             across to the foot of the stairs and calls in stentorian
             tones.*) Mary! There's a young man to see you about the
             electrics!

PETER   No, not the—oh never mind!

MRS. TRUDGE (*turning to* PETER) She'll be 'ere in a minute. Now, if
             you don't mind, some of us 'ave got a job of work to
             do. (*She limps painfully towards the kitchen with the
             tongs raised.*)

PETER   (*pointing to the tongs*) Fire gone out?

MRS. TRUDGE No, I got trouble with the fridge.

PETER   The fridge?

MRS. TRUDGE Yus. I lost me beads down the back. I'm trying to fish
             'em out.

PETER   (*taking a step forward*) Can I help?

MRS. TRUDGE (*pointing the tongs at him*) You stop 'ere. I don't want
             you tinkering around with my currents.

PETER   I wouldn't dream of it!

MRS. TRUDGE And don't you get up to any mischief until Miss Mary
             gets 'ere! (*She goes out to the kitchen and slams the
             door.*)

PETER   What a funny woman!
             (*He looks enquiringly round the room, and then inevit-
             ably goes for a closer look at the 'weighing machine'.
             He looks round furtively to make sure he is alone, fishes
             in his pocket for a penny, stands on the step in front of
             the machine and looks in vain for a slot to put his penny
             in. Deciding there isn't one he pushes a knob for the hell
             of it. A bell clangs and the pointer whirls wildly round
             and stops. Recovering from the shock* PETER *reads what
             it says.*)
             Three lemons!
             (*There is the jingle and crash of a jackpot being deliv-
             ered but nothing appears.* PETER *bends down and looks all*

round the machine hopefully. Then he steps off the plat-
form and stands with his back to it scratching his head.)
What a swizz!
(Suddenly the loud-speaker over the top comes to life
and speaks with a metallic voice not unlike a 'Speak
Your Weight' machine but a touch more authori-
tative.)

MACHINE Good evening!

PETER *(jumping forward two feet and whirling round)* What?
What?

MACHINE Mr. Shaw is out. Will you please put your hat on the
peg under the stairs.
(PETER looks round wildly then goes to the cupboard,
keeping a wary eye on the machine. He reaches up
obediently to his bare head.)

PETER Er—yes. Thank you—I haven't got a hat!

MACHINE Thank you. Mr. Shaw will return at nine o'clock. Do
you wish to leave a message?

PETER Yes—no. I don't think so. *(He comes back to the*
machine.)

MACHINE *(relentlessly)* If you wish to leave a message press the
red button and speak into the dial.
(PETER stands close, presses the button and shouts.)

PETER I do not wish to leave a message!

MACHINE I will convey that message to Mr. Shaw.

PETER That'll be great!

MACHINE Do not be alarmed. This is a recorded statement.

PETER Now he tells me.

MACHINE The weather forecast is windy and wet.

PETER *(pacing up and down)* It usually is.

MACHINE The toilet is outside in the hall, second on the right.

PETER *(glaring at the machine)* I don't wish to know that.
(The machine appears to have finished its repertoire and
PETER *goes to inspect it again.)*
Have you finished?

MACHINE At the third stroke it will be nine o'clock precisely.
(PETER staggers back and the machine emits three loud
pips.)

PETER I do wish you wouldn't do that! *(He goes to the stairs*
and looks up them hopefully.) Anyone about?

MACHINE (*inconsequentially*) The oyster season opens on August the fifth.

(PETER *flops down on the sofa and pretends to read a magazine, with his back to the machine.*

AUNT ESTHER *appears on the stairway, unnoticed by* PETER. *She is a woman of about 55, tall and imposing but quite definitely a little odd. She is given to 'causes' and is at present an ardent supporter of astrology and vegetarianism. She is strikingly clad in a long white evening gown, with her hair, slightly tinged with green, in a glittering silver Alice-band. She looks like a cross between a fairy godmother and one of the Muses. Seeing* PETER *she strikes a pose, hands outstretched and receptive, eyes closed. Her voice is deep and vibrant.*)

ESTHER You must be Leo the Lion.

PETER (*without turning*) Well, you're wrong there. I'm Mickey Mouse! (*He suddenly realises the voice is different, turns and sees* ESTHER.) Oh my gracious! (*He leaps to his feet and backs* D.L.)

ESTHER (*advancing D.C., arms outstretched*) Stand still! Let me feel your aura.

PETER What?

ESTHER (*standing in front of him with her arms outstretched an inch or so from his face*) Oh yes, quite definitely a Leo. Born?

PETER Yes, I think so. Oh yes, definitely.

ESTHER (*impatiently*) The date, the date!

PETER Let's see. It's May the fourth—no, the fifth.

ESTHER Young man, what is the date of your birthday?

PETER Oh sorry! August the fifth—the same day as the oysters.

ESTHER As I thought—a Leo. They always were an awkward lot!

MACHINE The following gale warning was issued at nineteen-thirty hours today. Finisterre, Biscay——

(ESTHER *walks across and silences it by pressing a button.*)

ESTHER Oh, do be quiet. Once it gets going it loses all sense of proportion. (*She returns to* PETER *and shakes hands with him.*) Good evening. I'm Esther Shaw—but you know that already.

PETER   Good evening. Actually I came to see——

ESTHER   (*sitting on the sofa*) Do sit down. I knew who you were as soon as I saw you.

PETER   You did? I don't think I——
         (ESTHER *draws him down beside her on the sofa and gazes raptly into his eyes.*)

ESTHER   Normally, of course, I don't see anyone in the evenings but this is rather special isn't it?

PETER   Is it? Actually I came to see Mary and——

ESTHER   When did you feel this coming on?

PETER   Coming on? You make it sound like the toothache.

ESTHER   I mean did it happen gradually or was it—cataclysmic?

PETER   Well, I don't really know. I was just standing there at the bus-stop and we got talking, you know how it is, and—well——

ESTHER   And suddenly you felt—transfigured!

PETER   Well, I wouldn't call it that exactly. Sort of peckish really. We both did, and so we went into that little café on the corner for a bite to eat and then——

ESTHER   Young man. What are you talking about?

PETER   Mary and me. I thought you wanted to know.

ESTHER   (*standing up*) I take it you are not Albert Shorter?

PETER   (*also standing*) Good lord, no! I'm Peter—Peter Puller.

ESTHER   And you did not come round to discuss a case of inter-corporeal transmigration?

PETER   I couldn't even pronounce it. No, I came to see Mary actually.

ESTHER   Most disappointing. (*She moves across* R.) I might have known it wouldn't happen to a Leo. (*She turns and points an accusing finger at* PETER.) Then what have you done with Mr. Shorter?

PETER   I haven't done anything with him!

ESTHER   But he said on the telephone he would come round this evening. A most remarkable case.

PETER   Perhaps he's—what you said—migrated.

ESTHER   (*looking at him solemnly and easing towards* C.) Do you study the stars?

PETER   (*moving towards her*) Oh yes. I know the Plough and Orion and Cassiopeia—that's the one like a W——

ESTHER   I am referring to the mystic power of the zodiac.

PETER What, Old Moore and all that stuff?

ESTHER Take care! The stars are watching. Your destiny is written there—up there.

(*She points aloft, a prophetess of doom, and* PETER *gazes vacantly at the ceiling. As they stand craning their necks upwards* MARY *appears from the stairs and marches briskly between them. She is 19, gay and pretty with a stubborn streak. She is wearing trews and a jumper.*)

MARY What's the matter, auntie? Have we sprung a leak?

ESTHER We have an unbeliever amongst us.

MARY Oh yes, I heard Mrs. Trudge call but I was in the bath. (*She turns to* PETER.) You've come about the electrics—Peter!

PETER Hallo, Mary.

MARY Peter darling, whatever are you doing here?

PETER (*glancing at* ESTHER) I don't quite know—now. I thought I came to see you.

MARY What have you been doing to Peter, auntie?

ESTHER How was I to know he was a friend of yours, dear? He was pretending to be Albert Shorter. (*She sits in the chair L. of table.*)

MARY Who?

PETER Albert Shorter. He's going to emigrate.

MARY Oh! Did you?

PETER What?

MARY Pretend to be Albert Whatsit?

PETER (*easing L.*) No, I don't think so.

ESTHER And he's a Leo too. Unreliable, Leos are.

MARY (*crossing to* ESTHER) Now look, auntie dear. Why don't you go and have a nice chat with Mrs. Trudge in the kitchen? She's very interested in horoscopes and things. She's a Sagittarian. (*She gives it a hard 'g'.*)

PETER Yes, she is a bit shapeless—it's probably the way her dress hangs.

ESTHER (*standing up*) No. Sagittarius. (*She pronounces it with a soft 'g'.*) The Archer, you know. They're very reliable, Sagittarians.

PETER That's good. You'll find her diving for pearls behind the fridge.

ESTHER Poor dear. She's getting a bit vague, you know. (*She goes towards the kitchen but turns and wags an admonitory finger.)* Now don't forget, young man, the stars have got their eyes on you. *(She sweeps magnificently out into the kitchen.)*

MARY   Sorry, I should have warned you about auntie.

PETER Yes, she is a bit overpowering.
       (MARY runs into his arms.)

MARY   Darling!

PETER *(Surprised.)* What? Oh yes. Darling!
       (They embrace but she suddenly breaks away and holds him at arm's length.)

MARY   But you shouldn't have come here.

PETER Why not?

MARY   You might meet daddy.

PETER But that's exactly why I've come. Best bib and tucker, see—and jolly uncomfortable it is too.

MARY   But he'll be terribly cross.

PETER Why? Doesn't he like collars and ties?

MARY   Silly! No, it's you.

PETER Now why should he be upset because you've got a boy-friend? Don't you think he'll approve of me? *(He kisses her ear reflectively.)*

MARY   Darling!

PETER Darling!
       (They embrace again.)

MARY   But he doesn't even know we're engaged.

PETER Neither did I. Good show!

MARY   Oo! I let that slip, didn't I? Well, we are engaged, aren't we? I mean sort of.

PETER Darling!
       (They sit on the sofa and cuddle close but just as PETER is getting enthusiastic MRS. TRUDGE enters from the kitchen and stands by the sofa glaring down at them. PETER, sensing trouble, breaks from his clinch.)
       Do you ever get the feeling you're being watched?
       (MRS. TRUDGE coughs and they spring apart.)

MRS. TRUDGE   'Ere, I thought you came round to see about the trouble with the electrics.

PETER Well—er—no. I—er—yes. That's to say——

MRS. TRUDGE   Wot you looking for then—loose connections?

PETER   I'm not looking for trouble.

MRS. TRUDGE   Not much you ain't! (*To* MARY.) You 'aven't come across
me beads in the excitement, I suppose?

MARY   No, Mrs. T. I'm sorry.

MRS. TRUDGE   (*humping back to the kitchen*) Well, don't let me inter-
rupt yer. 'Lectricians! Come in 'ere and start sparking
all over the sofa!
(*She goes out to the kitchen.* MARY *jumps to her feet.*)

MARY   It's no good, Peter. You'd better go.

PETER   But I've only just got here!

MARY   Daddy will have kittens if he finds you here.

PETER   But I still don't see why. I don't smoke. I don't drink—
much. And I change my socks every other day.

MARY   But you haven't got red hair.

PETER   What the devil has the colour of my hair got to do with
it?

MARY   Everything. Oh Peter, you must listen.

PETER   (*pulling her down on to the sofa again*) Come and sit
down, darling, and take it easy. You'll feel better in a
minute.

MARY   Oh, I do wish you'd listen! I told you before; daddy has
very strong ideas about the man I'm going to marry.

PETER   (*nuzzling her neck*) So have I.

MARY   But he has worked it all out scientifically. (*She clasps
her hands in her lap and drones out the following like
a catechism.*) Aged thirty, five feet eight inches, C. of E.,
blue eyes, red hair, spectacles and a tidy mind!

PETER   That sounds like a short-sighted waste-paper basket.
What's it supposed to be?

MARY   That, my poor darling, is the man I'm going to marry.
Fred says so.

PETER   Who?

MARY   Fred.

PETER   And who the devil is Fred?

MARY   (*pointing to the 'weighing machine'*) That is. He's a
computer. Frequency Regulated Electronic Device.
F-R-E-D. See?

PETER   (*walking up to take another look at* FRED) So that's
what it is. I thought it was a dehydrated butler. Well,
he's not a very good computer——

MARY But——

PETER ——Because I'm twenty-five, five feet ten, brown eyes, black hair and I'm a Bush Baptist. (*He goes up to the dial and snaps his fingers at it.*) So you can stick that up your fuse-box and blow it!
(FRED *lets out a loud raspberry and* PETER *staggers back.*)
That thing's damn near human!

MARY (*getting up and joining him*) Daddy made it. He says it's infallible. And if Fred reckons my husband is going to have red hair that's the way it's got to be. (*She runs her fingers through* PETER's *hair.*)

PETER (*stamping down stage*) Well, you can tell that heap of wires it had better start computing again because you're marrying me.
(*He sweeps her back on to the sofa and kisses her.*)

MARY Darling!

FRED (*interrupting their blissful moment with a snort*) In the event of fire, please leave by the Emergency Exit.
(PETER *tries to get up but* MARY *pulls him back.*)

PETER (*stroking her face*) What lovely soft skin.

FRED The average human skin contains two and a half million pores.

PETER What?

FRED Pores.

PETER Oh lord, I can't concentrate with him in the room. Fancy having your love life ruined by a ruddy robot!
(*He jumps to his feet and peers at the machine.*)
How does it work anyway? It looks like a weighing machine.

MARY The main works are in there, in daddy's laboratory. (*She points to the door marked 'Private'*) And there's some more under the stairs. Lots of black boxes and wires and things. This part is just daddy's idea of a joke. He records messages to surprise people.

PETER It certainly surprised me. Come to think of it your dad must have a funny voice.

MARY It's not him, it's Fred. Some of his wires are a bit tight.

PETER What happens if I press this? (*He points to the blue knob.*)

MARY Try it and see.

(PETER *presses the blue knob and the machine coughs into life.*)

FRED Prune juice and scrambled eggs.

PETER That's nice.

MARY It's the menu for breakfast tomorrow. He makes them up every day.

PETER Sounds delicious. Does he cook too?

MARY No, silly. (*She moves above sofa.*) Of course we shan't actually have it. At any rate I shan't. That's just what Fred reckons we need to give us our vitamins. Daddy does his best but he had to give in yesterday tea-time —tripe and charcoal biscuits!

PETER Sounds awful.

MARY Daddy said there must have been a vibration in his oscillator.

PETER Nasty!

MARY It's a sort of electronic burp.

PETER I don't wonder on a diet like that.

FRED Will you please put your hat on the peg under the stairs. (PETER *goes obediently towards the cupboard but stops short again.*)

PETER (*petulantly*) We've been through all that once!

MARY (*switching* FRED *off*) Darling, I think you'd better go before they come home. (*She crosses and takes his arm.*)

PETER Who? Oh, your parents. Where are they by the way?

MARY (*walking him* D.C.) Daddy's been lecturing. He's quite famous, you know. He often gets invited to talk about his old computers and mummy usually drives him to make sure he gets there. Dear old dad, he's terribly absent-minded.

PETER Do you think he might forget about the red hair?

MARY Not likely. He's got it written down. You must go. Please, darling.

PETER Oh well, if you think so.

MARY Yes, I do. (*She steers him towards the kitchen door.*) And you'd better go out the back way.

PETER Oh all right, but I still think it's a lot of nonsense. (*As they approach the door it is flung open and* ESTHER *enters, arms outstretched, followed by* MRS. TRUDGE. MARY *and* PETER *back away* L.)

ESTHER We've got them!

PETER You're telling me!

ESTHER Mrs. Trudge's beads. They weren't behind the fridge after all.

MRS. TRUDGE (*holding up the beads triumphantly*) I'd dropped 'em in a pie dish.

PETER That'll be nice for daddy's dinner. I hope somebody has told Fred.

ESTHER Ah! The bogus Mr. Shorter.
(*She crosses* MARY *and bears down on* PETER *who backs further away* D.L.)

MRS. TRUDGE Well, I can't stop 'ere gossiping. I got things to do.

PETER Dunking your garters in the gravy for instance.

MRS. TRUDGE (*calling across to* PETER) Found the trouble then?

PETER Oh yes, I've found trouble all right.

MRS. TRUDGE (*jerking her thumb at* FRED) Unnatural, that's what it is. Electrics leaking about all over the 'ouse. Don't do the paint no good neither.

MARY Thank you, Mrs. Trudge.

ESTHER And don't forget what I told you, dear. Be prepared for a big surprise tonight.

MRS. TRUDGE Oh yes. Me old man is going to wash 'is feet I shouldn't wonder. (*She goes out to the kitchen.*)

ESTHER Sometimes I feel Mrs. Trudge doesn't really appreciate the power of the cosmic forces. (*She turns to* PETER.) Well, young man, I hope you haven't been leading Mary astray?

PETER What? Oh no.

MARY (*coming to* ESTHER's *side*) He was just going, weren't you, Peter?

PETER Was I? (*He catches* MARY's *eye.*) Oh yes, that's right.

ESTHER You're sure you wouldn't like me to tell your fortune before you go?

PETER Some other time perhaps.
(*The front-door bell rings.*)

MARY Oh dear, that must be them.

ESTHER All right, dear, I'll answer it. (*She shouts loudly by* PETER's *ear.*) All right, Mrs. Trudge. I'll go!
(ESTHER *goes into the hall leaving* PETER *rubbing his ear.*)

PETER Does she ever shatter her crystal ball?

MARY (*pulling him towards the kitchen door*) Quick, darling, I'll see you tomorrow.

PETER I still don't see why——

(MARY *silences him with a kiss.*)

MARY 'Bye now.

(PETER *goes into the kitchen but a second later comes charging back again.*)

PETER They're coming in the back way. (*He starts to rush up the stairs.*)

MARY No, not up there. In here—quick.

(*She pushes him towards the cupboard under the stairs. He stops and points to the notice but she only shakes her head. He opens the door and is enveloped in an avalanche of hats.*)

PETER You seem to have had a lot of visitors!

(MARY *pushes him in, throws the hats in after him and pushes the door shut. He re-appears with a handful of wires.*)

I seem to have walked through some wires.

MARY Oh, never mind that now.

(PETER *returns to hiding just as* GEORGE SHAW *enters from the kitchen. He is a man of about 50 and looks the boffin he is. Carelessly dressed and rather shaggy round the ears, he has a habit of looking over the top of his spectacles when trying to concentrate. He is wearing an open overcoat.*)

GEORGE (*below the table*) Ah! There you are, Mary.

(MARY *jumps and shoves the cupboard door shut.*)

MARY Oh hallo, daddy! (*She moves guiltily D.R. away from the cupboard.*)

GEORGE (*moving D.C.*) Had to come round the back—forgot the door key. (*He pats the computer affectionately.*) 'Evening, Fred. (*To* MARY.) Where's your mother?

MARY I thought she was with you.

GEORGE Oh yes, so she was. I'd better let her in.

(*He moves towards the hall door just as* MARJORIE SHAW *enters followed by* ESTHER. MARJORIE *is a pleasant, good-natured woman a few years younger than* GEORGE *and this helps her to survive and even bring a sense of order into this extraordinary household. She is wearing a light coat and carrying gloves and handbag.*)

Oh, there you are, dear. Hallo, Esther, I didn't know you'd been out. You want to wrap up a bit warmer. These May evenings can be a bit nippy.

(ESTHER *turns her eyes up to the ceiling in despair.* MARJORIE *crosses to* MARY.)

MARJORIE Hallo, darling. Everything all right? (*She puts her hand-bag and gloves on the table.*)

MARY Fine, thanks.

ESTHER (*from D.L.*) What's happened to the other Mr. Shorter?

GEORGE Who?

ESTHER Albert Shorter. I was just going to tell him about the stars.

GEORGE Poor devil!

(MARJORIE *takes off her coat and moves towards the cupboard.*)

ESTHER And now he seems to have disappeared. A very strange young man.

(ESTHER *sits on the sofa.* MARY *moves up to head* MARJORIE *off before she gets to the cupboard.*)

MARY He—er—he had to go home suddenly.

GEORGE Got taken shorter, eh? (*He turns his attention to* FRED.)

(PETER's *head appears.* MARY *waves him in and he waves amiably back.*)

FRED Try the cupboard.

GEORGE What?

FRED He's hanging his hat in the cupboard.

MARY (*To* FRED) Ssh!

GEORGE I do believe Fred's trying to tell me something.

ESTHER Rubbish!

MARY Oh, really, daddy!

GEORGE (*darkly*) You never know.

MARY Let me take your coat, mummy.

MARJORIE Oh, thank you, dear.

(*She gives* MARY *her coat and crosses D.R.*)

Cup of tea, George?

GEORGE No, just a drop of oil, I think.

ESTHER Oil!

GEORGE Yes, the pointer's sticking again.

ESTHER Oh, you and that blessed computer!

MARJORIE Take your coat off, dear, I'll go and make some tea. I expect Mrs. Trudge will have the kettle on. Like a cup, Mary?

MARY No thanks. You never know what's been in the kettle.

MARJORIE Esther?

ESTHER You know very well, dear. I never touch stimulants.

GEORGE (*apparently addressing* FRED) Just as well. She's like a flea in a fit as it is. (*He meanders towards the cupboard taking off his coat.*)

MARJORIE (*heading for the kitchen*) I shan't be long. (*She goes out.*)

ESTHER Just because I have the misfortune to be your sister there is no reason to be rude.

MARY (*helping* GEORGE *off with his coat*) Let me help, daddy.

GEORGE We are attentive tonight. (*To* ESTHER.) Don't take any notice of me, Esther. I'm just not in the mood for star-gazing this evening—night starvation I dare say.
(*He notices* MARY, *who is standing holding the coats in front of the cupboard.*)
Well, go on, put them away.
(MARY *shuffles the cupboard door open and pushes the coats in round the side, smiling brightly.* PETER *whips them smartly inside.*)
Thank you. That should do them the world of good!
(*He crosses to the sideboard and starts to tinker with the works of the clock.* PETER *peers out.*)

ESTHER (*patting the sofa*) Is everything all right, Mary? You're looking a little pale, my child.

MARY (*walking down* C.) Everything's fine.

ESTHER That young man didn't bother you?

MARY No, no!

GEORGE (*taking a screw-driver from his pocket*) Young man. What young man?

ESTHER The one masquerading as Albert Shorter.

GEORGE (*busy with the clock*) What did he want?

MARY Oh, he—er—came round about the electrics.

GEORGE I didn't know there was anything wrong with them. I must have a look at once.
(*He makes for the cupboard and* PETER *disappears smartly.* MARY *heads* GEORGE *off.*)

MARY No, it was the wrong number—I mean wrong house.

ESTHER It took him long enough to find out. A thoroughly unreliable young man if you ask me.

GEORGE I hope he wasn't a burglar. What did he look like?

MARY (*casually*) I hardly noticed.

FRED Brown hair, black eyes and a dirty collar.

MARY Shush!

FRED Mind like a waste-paper basket.

MARY (*thumping* FRED) Will you be quiet!

ESTHER I think we ought to count the spoons. Do you know
he wouldn't even let me tell his fortune.

GEORGE Well, that's something in his favour.

ESTHER (*rising haughtily*) Oh well, if you feel like that I shall
go to my room.

GEORGE (*putting the clock back on the sideboard*) Good night,
Esther. Don't drop your ouija board again tonight. It's
bad for my nerves.

ESTHER Philistine! (*She moves to* MARY *and kisses her on the
cheek.*) Good night, Mary, my poor child.

MARY Good night, auntie. Sleep tight.

ESTHER I shan't sleep a wink. You know how sensitive I am
when the moon is on the wane.

GEORGE You snore like a fog-horn whether it's waning or snow-
ing.
(ESTHER *leaves up the stairs with a toss of her head.*)
(*Calling after her.*) And if you must go out digging for
hemlock at midnight don't do it in the middle of my
lawn. Now then. (*He goes to* FRED.) Let's see what else
you've got to say for yourself. (*He pushes a knob and
there is a loud buzz but nothing else happens.*)
That's funny. Must have blown a fuse. Never mind,
we'll soon fix that.
(*He walks towards the cupboard and again* MARY *intercepts him in the nick of time. She links arms and leads
him* D.C.)

MARY Oh, you don't want to worry about your old computer
tonight, daddy. Let's—er—let's have a game of scrabble.

GEORGE I thought you hated it.

MARY Well, I might have grown to like it.

GEORGE What, since last night? No dear, never re-fuse tomorrow
what you can re-fuse today. I say, that's rather good.

MARY Hmmm!

(GEORGE *tries to pass her.*)

Let me do it for you.

GEORGE I didn't know you were interested.

MARY (*leading him* D.R.) Oh yes, jolly interested. I just love those wriggly little electrons. Tell me all about it.

GEORGE Well, you see the whole thing works on the binary principle—no, you wouldn't understand. (*He sidesteps* MARY *and walks to the cupboard door with* MARY *chasing after him.*) I must mend that fuse.

(*He opens the door and exposes* PETER *with his eyes tight shut wearing two or three hats and still holding his heap of wires. Luckily* MARJORIE *enters from the kitchen at that moment with two cups of tea and distracts* GEORGE's *attention from the cupboard.*)

MARJORIE Here we are. Tea up!

(*She puts the tea down on the table.* PETER *hastily pulls the cupboard door shut again, snatching the handle out of* GEORGE's *hand.* GEORGE *looks at it over the top of his spectacles in some surprise.*)

GEORGE There must be a draught in here tonight.

MARY (*getting between* GEORGE *and the cupboard*) Oh yes, there is! You'd be much better off in bed.

MARJORIE (*handing* GEORGE *a cup of tea and sitting at the table*) You seem to be in a hurry to get rid of us, Mary.

GEORGE (*jocularly*) You know what it is, mother. She's trying to hide something. (*He sits with his tea on the sofa.*)

(MARJORIE *picks up a newspaper from the table, puts on her spectacles and starts to read.*)

Isn't that right?

MARY No, no!

(*There is a loud sneeze from the cupboard.*)

FRED Bless you!

GEORGE What was that?

MARJORIE Fred.

GEORGE No, no. Somebody sneezed.

MARJORIE Perhaps he's caught a chill in his choke.

MARY I didn't hear anything. Let's have some music.

(*She switches on the radio on the sideboard. The room is filled with pop music.*)

GEORGE I tell you I heard a sneeze.

(*Another sneeze.* MARY *turns the volume up.*)

There you are. There it is again. Oh for heaven's sake!
(*The radio blares out even louder.* GEORGE *jumps to his
feet and marches across to switch it off.* MARY *comes
to meet him and leads him into an extravagant dance,
tea and all. After a quick turn round the room he breaks
free and manages to switch off the radio.*)

Really, I don't know what's the matter with you tonight.

MARY Oh, don't be an old square, dad. (*She creeps up to listen
at the cupboard without making it too obvious.*) That
was radio Lulu.

GEORGE Lulu's about right.

MARY Doesn't it send you?

GEORGE (*moving to* C.) Yes, it sends me crazy. And there's no
need to look so innocent. I know when somebody's trying to change the subject. There's something very fishy
going on. Now why should the computer choose tonight
to peter out?

MARJORIE (*looking up from her newspaper*) Do what, dear?

GEORGE (*loudly*) Peter out!

(*The cupboard door opens and* PETER *duly appears.*
GEORGE *and* MARJORIE *both have their backs turned and*
MARY *manages to shuffle him back inside and stand with
her back against the door.* GEORGE *jumps as the door
slams shut.*)

What on earth!

(PETER *tries hard to open the door and* MARY *keeps
jumping forward a couple of feet as he pushes and then
forces the door back again.*)

What are you doing?

MARY It's a new—dance! Called the—jerk! Got—words—
too—— (*She shouts out in time to the jerking.*) Stop—
pushing—and don't be—vicious! Mummy and—daddy
are—getting sus—picious!

(PETER *takes the hint and* MARY *subsides.*)

GEORGE (*shaking his head sadly*) I don't know what young
people are coming to. It's all this television.

MARJORIE You're a fine one to talk! You know all the adverts off
by heart.

GEORGE Oh, that reminds me. (*He looks over* MARJORIE's *shoulder at the paper.*) I see they've got my advertisement in the local paper.

MARY What advertisement?

GEORGE (*picking up the paper and moving* C.) Excuse me, dear. Let's see now. Ah yes, here it is.
(GEORGE *points with his finger and* MARY *reads.*)

MARY 'Wanted. Scientific assistant for interesting and profitable situation. Good prospects. Red hair and good figurework essential. Apply 26 Walnut Grove.' That's here.

GEORGE What about that, my girl? That should bring the young men running. Then you can take your pick.
(*He unexpectedly smacks* MARY *on the bottom with the paper. She snatches it from him.*)

MARY I keep telling you I'm allergic to red hair! (*She moves* D.L., *re-reading the advert to herself.*)

GEORGE Nonsense! Fred never fails.

MARY Well, he's failed now.

GEORGE A mere technical hitch. Let me just mend that fuse——
(*He goes towards the cupboard again and* MARY *runs* U.L. *and intercepts him.*)

MARY No, I will.

GEORGE Well, all right. As you're so keen. I'll be in the workshop if anyone wants me. (*He goes out to the laboratory.*)

MARY (*crossing to* MARJORIE) Oh! It's worse than the slave market.

MARJORIE (*looking up from the magazine she is reading*) What is, dear?

MARY This advert. (*Holding out the paper.*) It's positively feudal.

MARJORIE (*reading*) 'Will exchange goldfish for eight-day chiming clock.' I didn't know we had a goldfish.

MARY No, not that. This one here. (*She points.*)

MARJORIE (*reading*) Oh that! I shouldn't worry. It'll all turn out for the best.

MARY But I want to marry Peter.

MARJORIE Who, dear?

MARY Peter. You know, I told you.

MARJORIE Oh, the boy you met at the bus-stop. Yes, you must bring him round some time. I'd like to meet him.

MARY (*pointing*) He's in the cubby-hole.

MARJORIE Oh dear. I haven't dusted under there for weeks. You'd better let him out. (*She stands.*)

MARY Only if you promise not to tell daddy.

MARJORIE That's very deceitful. But I know just what you mean. All right then.

MARY Cub's honour?

MARJORIE (*giving a cub salute*) Dyb, dyb, dyb.
(*MARY opens the cupboard door and PETER emerges looking a little crumpled and wearing a very large bowler hat which comes down to his ears.*)

MARY (*on his left*) Mummy, this is Peter.

MARJORIE (*moving to PETER*) How do you do? I'm so pleased to meet you.

PETER Good evening.
(*He raises his bowler, replaces it and virtually extinguishes himself and they shake hands.*)

GEORGE (*off*) Mary! Marjorie!

MARY Quick. Back you go.

PETER But I say!
(*One on each side they stuff him protesting back into the cupboard and shut the door just as GEORGE appears from the lab. They stand looking sheepish.*)

GEORGE What are you two up to under there?

MARJORIE Just putting a shilling in the Peter—I mean the meter.

GEORGE But it's not that sort of meter.

MARY No wonder we couldn't find the slot.

GEORGE Well, just leave it for a minute, will you, and lend me a hand in here. My voltages are falling again.

MARJORIE How undignified.
(*The front door bell rings.*)

MARY There's the bell. (*She moves U.L.*)

GEORGE I know, I know. But this is serious. Leave it to Mrs. Trudge. (*He shouts.*) Mrs. Trudge—shop!

MARY But daddy!

GEORGE Now come along, come along, that'll keep.
(*MARY and MARJORIE shrug at one another and troop obediently after GEORGE into the lab and close the door. As they disappear MRS. TRUDGE enters from the kitchen and limps across muttering.*)

MRS. TRUDGE That's right, you lazy lot of lumps. Don't you bother to answer it. I 'aven't got anything better to do, I suppose. Caught me right in the middle of me Instant Whip.

(*As she goes out into the hall* PETER *emerges stealthily from the cupboard and looks carefully round. He puts the bowler hat on to the bust on the sideboard and pulls a face at* FRED.)

PETER Red hair, eh? You—you refugee from a fun-fair. We'll see about that.

(*He starts towards the hall but, hearing voices, dives for the shelter of the window recess and hides behind the curtains D.L.* MRS. TRUDGE *enters from the hall followed by* ALBERT SHORTER, *a small, unhappy little man who wears his trousers hoisted too high.*)

MRS. TRUDGE You better wait 'ere, Mr. Shorter. They're all in there giving Mr. Shaw a 'elping 'and. They'll be out in a bit.

ALBERT Is he unwell?

MRS. TRUDGE (*in a hoarse whisper*) It's 'is brain. Gone wrong again, I expect.

ALBERT Dear me.

MRS. TRUDGE (*darkly*) It's the hozone what does it. You mark my words.

(*She goes to the kitchen and* ALBERT *patrols the room with some deference. He inspects the bowler-hatted bust and comes to an abrupt halt in front of* FRED. *Suddenly* MARJORIE *enters from the lab, closing the door after her. She has slipped her spectacles into her pocket.*)

MARJORIE Ah, you shouldn't be out here, Peter.

ALBERT I'm Shorter.

MARJORIE (*looking him up and down*) Yes, you are a bit. It must be the damp weather. It makes everything shrink. Quick, he's coming!

ALBERT But—but——

(*She propels him backwards into the cupboard and shuts the door just as* GEORGE *and* MARY *enter from the lab.*)

GEORGE So you see it can't possibly go wrong.

MARY (*looking anxiously at* MARJORIE) But daddy——

GEORGE (*patting her arm*) I know, I know. It always comes as a bit of a shock when we find out who we're going to marry. I always used to come up in a rash whenever

I got near your mother. But it'll work out and you'll
thank your old dad one day.

(MARJORIE *makes signs to* MARY *over* GEORGE's *head to
indicate that* PETER *is safely in the cupboard.* PETER's
*head appears through the curtains and he tries to attract
their attention.*)

Just think of it—the perfect match. It's like——

MARJORIE Tripe and onions.

GEORGE Yes—no! Romeo and Juliet.

MARY But he didn't have red hair.

GEORGE No, but you see in his case—— (*He spots* MARJORIE
making signs.) What are you doing?

(PETER *ducks out of sight and* MARJORIE *pretends to be
smoothing her hair straight.*)

MARJORIE Nothing, dear. You just carry on computering.

GEORGE You two are up to something. You're looking a sight
too innocent for my liking.

MARJORIE Ah, but you're forgetting what tomorrow is.

GEORGE No, I'm not—it's Tuesday. Andy Pandy's on. (*He moves
D.C.*)

MARJORIE And what else?

GEORGE (*hopefully*) The Flintstones? No, they're on Mondays.

MARJORIE It's your birthday.

GEORGE By george, so it is! I'm glad you reminded me. I must
wind the clock.

MARY (*moving to* GEORGE) So don't you think you ought to
get in an early night, daddy? You'll need all your energy
opening parcels in the morning.

GEORGE (*looking at his watch*) But it's only half-past nine.

MARJORIE Well, I think an early night would do us all good. Esther
seems to have gone up already.

GEORGE She's nothing to go by. She sits up there half the night
knitting spells and reading runes.

MARY It's called 'Fanny Hill'.

GEORGE What is?

MARY Her latest rune. She keeps it under the bed. It's a rude
rune.

MARJORIE You're not supposed to know about things like that.

MARY Oh mummy dear, you're a scream. We took it for G.C.E.

GEORGE Well anyway, I refuse to go to bed until I've finished this chapter. (*He crosses to sofa, sits down and starts to read his library book.*)

MARJORIE (*leaning over the back of the sofa and stroking his forehead*) It would smooth out all those tired little wrinkles.

GEORGE It hasn't done Esther much good. All her little wrinkles are yawning their heads off.

(*He resumes his reading.* MARY *creeps back to the cupboard door and listens. She makes a sign to* MARJORIE *who joins her just as* PETER *reaches out from the curtains and tries to attract her attention. He almost falls on to the sofa beside* GEORGE *and beats a hasty retreat.*)

MARY (*whispering to* MARJORIE) It's all right, I can't hear anything.

PETER Pssst!

GEORGE (*looking up*) What's that?

(PETER's *head disappears again.*)

MARJORIE Nothing, dear. Mary says she can't hear anything.

GEORGE She'd better go round to Doctor Lane in the morning and have her ears seen to.

(GEORGE *returns to his book. The two women bend down and listen at the cupboard door. Unseen by them* GEORGE *creeps up behind and listens too.* PETER *emerges from hiding and starts to creep across towards the kitchen door. Suddenly* GEORGE *bangs his book shut with a loud crash.* PETER *jumps three feet into the air and dives back behind the curtains.* MARY *and* MARJORIE *scream and jump apart.*)

You heard that all right.

MARY Oh, daddy!

MARJORIE George, if you ever do that again I'll divorce you.

(*She sits L. of the table to recover. From the cupboard comes a strangled moan.*)

GEORGE What was that?

MARY (*hopefully*) I didn't hear anything. (*She walks across to the sideboard.*)

GEORGE Oh, don't start that again. It came from in here.

(*He taps a tattoo on the cupboard door—Da di di da dit. And the cupboard taps back—Da da.*)

Good lord! We've got the beetles. (*He calls.*) Mrs. Trudge!

MARY   Oh, Peter, you idiot.
        (*The idiot makes defensive faces between the curtains
        but fails to attract any attention.*)

MARJORIE   Mary!

MARY   It's no good, mummy, the cat's out of the bag. We may
        as well let him know. (*She walks across to the cup-
        board.*) Daddy, I'd like you to meet Peter. (*She throws
        the door open.*) We're going to be married.
        (ALBERT *steps out looking dishevelled with a bunch of
        wires in his hands like headless flowers.*)
        Oh!
        (*She retreats hastily to stand behind* MARJORIE'*s chair.*)

GEORGE   (*calmly shaking* ALBERT'*s hand*) How do you do?

ALBERT   How—how—I—who?

GEORGE   I'm George Shaw, Mary's father.
         (MRS. TRUDGE *limps muttering across between* GEORGE
         and ALBERT *and out into the hall. She shakes* ALBERT'*s
         hand as she passes.*)

MARY   (*to* MARJORIE) Who's this?

MARJORIE   It's Peter. Don't you remember?

MARY   No it isn't!

MARJORIE   (*putting on her spectacles*) Isn't it? So it isn't. Never
         mind, as long as you're in love that's the main thing.

MARY   But mummy!

GEORGE   (*pointing to* ALBERT'*s bunch of wires*) You interested in
         computers?

ALBERT   Not very. I came to see Miss Shaw.

GEORGE   So I gather. Don't be shy, you can call her Mary.
         (*He pushes* ALBERT *towards* MARY.)

ALBERT   I thought her name was Esther.

GEORGE   You don't know one another very well, do you? Esther
         is my sister. Like to meet her? (*He goes to the foot of
         the stairs.*) Esther! She'll be down in a bit. (*He returns
         D.L.*)

MARY   But, daddy, I wish you'd listen——

MARJORIE   I do think you might have left Esther in peace.

GEORGE   Nonsense. Do her good to have a bit of company. Stuck
         up there in bed with Old Moore all night long.
         (MRS. TRUDGE *re-enters and comes to* ALBERT'*s side.*)

MRS. TRUDGE   There wasn't no one there.

ALBERT What?

MRS. TRUDGE Nobody there, there wasn't. You got bells in yer 'ead, you 'ave. (*She limps out into the kitchen.*)

ALBERT What was that about?

MARJORIE Goodness knows. She's getting a bit absent-minded.

MARY Daddy, I wish you'd let me explain.

GEORGE (*inspecting the wires* ALBERT *is holding*) In a minute, dear. These are the very things I've been looking for. Where did you come across these?

ALBERT I just found them lying around.

GEORGE Let me introduce you.
(*He leads* ALBERT *towards* MARJORIE, *who rises and gets her best smile ready until* GEORGE *walks right past and up to the computer.*)
This is Fred.

ALBERT What?

GEORGE Fred.

ALBERT Oh!

GEORGE (*going to the stairs and shouting*) Esther!
(MARJORIE *nudges him in the back.*)
Hmm? Oh and this is Fred's mother. (*He turns back to the machine.*) You see it works on the binary principle——

MARJORIE (*to* ALBERT) I'm Mrs. Shaw—Mary's mother. (*She shakes* ALBERT's *hand.*)

GEORGE (*continuing unaware*) The input is in the other room and under here—— (*He walks across to the cupboard.*)

MARJORIE And this is Mary.

ALBERT How do you do? (*He shakes* MARY's *hand.*)

GEORGE (*to* ALBERT) Are you listening, young man? What's your name?

ALBERT Albert—Albert Shorter.

GEORGE Not *the* Albert Shorter?

ALBERT Hmm?

GEORGE Never mind. I suppose you'll be expecting to call me father.

ALBERT But I——

GEORGE Well, don't count on it. Your hair's the wrong colour.
(ESTHER *appears on the stairs. She is dressed in a magni-*

ficent nightdress and night-cap and her hands are stretched out in front of her like a sleep-walker.)

ESTHER Someone calls.

GEORGE Oh, there you are, Esther. I want you to meet——

ESTHER Someone is calling——

(*She advances slowly D.C., arms outstretched, between* MARJORIE *and* GEORGE.)

GEORGE (*petulantly*) Oh, nobody's listening to me this evening.

MARJORIE Oh dear, she's having one of her turns again.

(ESTHER *sweeps on until she stands in front of the curtains D.L.*)

ESTHER There is a presence in the room.

(*She suddenly throws open the curtains and finds herself face to face with* POPPY BLOSSOM. *The french windows behind* POPPY *are open and* PETER *is nowhere to be seen.* POPPY *is an attractive young woman of about 25. She is dressed in a smart but business-like costume with a high-necked blouse. Her red hair is drawn back in a knot and she wears cat-shaped spectacles. The whole effect is of an efficient young woman with a good deal more to commend her than her shorthand. She carries a small attaché case.*)

GEORGE Who on earth?

(POPPY *advances to C. and puts down her case.*)

POPPY I believe you wanted a red-haired assistant.

QUICK CURTAIN

ACT II

The same. Breakfast time next morning. A pot of tea, milk jug, sugar basin, cups and saucers stand on the sideboard with a large packet of cornflakes. On the table a cloth, cereal plates, knives, forks and spoons, toast and marmalade. In the centre a big bowl of fruit—apples and bananas—and a vase of flowers.

The curtains are open and the sun is shining outside. Regardless of the weather the bust of Plato or whoever it is still wears the bowler hat and a white laboratory coat is draped across the back of the sofa.

GEORGE is seated above the table and ESTHER is sitting L. of table. Both are reading. GEORGE has the Times and ESTHER is immersed in a magazine.

GEORGE is dressed in comfortable casual clothes. ESTHER is wearing a colourful floral dressing-gown and fluffy slippers. Her spectacles are perched on the end of her nose and she is peeling an apple without paying very much attention.

Suddenly ESTHER looks up and points her knife at GEORGE.

ESTHER George! Are you a Virgin or a Ram?

GEORGE (looking up startled) What?

ESTHER A Virgin or a Ram? I can never remember.

(MARJORIE enters from the kitchen in time to hear the end of the conversation. She is quietly dressed in a summer dress with an apron on top. She is carrying a large tray with a kipper on a plate.)

MARJORIE He's a Goat.

(MARJORIE puts the tray down on the table.)

ESTHER Most appropriate.

GEORGE Well, you're both wrong. I happen to be a Bull.

MARJORIE I knew it was something with horns.

ESTHER Well now, let's see. Taurus, Taurus—— (She runs the knife down the page.) Oh yes, here we are. (Reads.) 'Mars is in the ascendant——'

MARJORIE And Mary is still in the bathroom. (*She goes to the foot of the stairs.*)

ESTHER That's a bad sign!

GEORGE Oh, I don't know. It's better than being dirty.

ESTHER I meant Mars.

MARJORIE (*calling*) Mary! Breakfast!

ESTHER (*reading*) 'Jupiter and Saturn are in conjunction——'

GEORGE (*reading*) 'The Tories have won the by-election at Cheltenham——'

MARJORIE (*returning to the table*) And the bacon's gone spotty again.

ESTHER (*louder*) 'The moon is in the House of Pisces.'

GEORGE (*about to read but unable to believe his ears*) What?

ESTHER Pisces—the fish. The sign of the fish.

(MARJORIE *puts the kipper down in front of* GEORGE.)

GEORGE What's this?

MARJORIE Kipper, dear.

GEORGE What again? We had Pisces yesterday.

MARJORIE I know, dear, but the bacon's gone spotty. I told you.

ESTHER (*sternly*) Do you want to hear your fortune or not?

GEORGE No!

ESTHER It says here a day for surprises but you must beware of romantic indiscretions.

GEORGE Chance would be a fine thing.

MARJORIE Is that the Miss Chance in the paper shop? (*She pours two cups of tea.*)

GEORGE Mischance is right! She's sixty if she's a day and she's got a moustache like Jimmy Edwards.

MARJORIE Poor woman. She can't help her looks.

GEORGE Maybe not but she can help sending me 'Chicks Own' instead of 'The Economist'. (*He holds up the offending comic.*)

ESTHER She studies her customers if you ask me.

GEORGE Well, you study your stars and tell us what they've got in store for Marjorie. She's an old Aquarius.

ESTHER (*running her finger down the page*) Aquarius?—Oh yes. (*Reads.*) 'Best behaviour today and follow the party line.'

GEORGE Love, honour and obey, eh? That's more like it.

(MARJORIE *hands him a cup of tea and sits table* R. *drinking her own.*)

By the way, I thought Fred said we should be having scrambled eggs for breakfast.

MARJORIE Well, he'd better start laying the eggs then because we haven't got any.

GEORGE You see! No co-operation. (*To* ESTHER.) Is that all?

ESTHER No. It says, 'Expect a dark stranger.'

GEORGE It would.

(*There is a ring at the front door.*)

ESTHER There!

MARJORIE That'll be the postman. (*She goes out to the hall.*)

GEORGE (*busy with his kipper*) I don't know how you can bother with that nonsense, Esther.

ESTHER It's very scientific. Doctor Cosmos never lies.

GEORGE Who?

ESTHER Doctor Cosmos. (*Reads.*) 'Astrologer extraordinary by appointment.'

(GEORGE *laughs.*)

Oh, you can laugh. (*Darkly.*) But you wait and see. (*She reads again.*) 'A day for surprises.'

(MARY *enters down the stairs dressed in a skirt and jumper.*)

MARY Hallo, daddy dear. Happy birthday. (*She kisses him on top of his head and gives him a small parcel.*)

GEORGE Hallo, what's this?

MARY Just a little surprise.

(GEORGE *looks at* ESTHER *who puts on a smug expression.* MARY *kisses her on the cheek.*)

'Morning, auntie. What's news?

ESTHER Good morning, Mary dear. I was just warning your father not to mock at the unknown.

GEORGE Takes me all my time to keep up with what I do know.

MARY (*helping herself to cornflakes and tea*) What have you been up to now?

GEORGE (*fighting with the parcel*) I was merely pointing out to your aunt—I wish you wouldn't use so much sticky tape—that in these days of scientific progress I refuse to accept—(*He opens the parcel and reveals a pair of purple socks.*) Good Lord! Thank you, dear. Just what I wanted. I say I refuse to accept a lot of mediaeval mumbo-jumbo.

(FRED *emits three loud pips and buzzes to life.*)

FRED   Good morning. Today is the sixth of May—the thir-
teenth day of Ramadan. (*He bursts into song.*) Happy
birthday to you. Happy birthday to you.
(MARY *joins in.*)
Happy birthday, dear daddy/George, happy birthday to
you.

GEORGE   Thank you, Fred. Thank you, dear.

FRED   The temperature this morning is thirteen degrees Centi-
grade. Do not remove your winter vest.

MARY   Ne'er cast a clout till May be out. I wonder what that
really means.

FRED   Barometric pressure one thousand and twelve millibars——
(ESTHER *turns* FRED *off with a jab of her thumb.*)

ESTHER   Oh do be quiet! Those millibars always make me feel
itchy. And talking about mumbo-jumbo, what about
this? (*She points at the machine.*)

GEORGE   Fred? What about him?

ESTHER   (*sitting down again.*) Oh, it's a him now, is it? I suppose
you call that being scientific.

GEORGE   Certainly. He thinks like a man. Cool, calm and logical.
None of this emotional guess-work you women call in-
tuition. That's why he's always right.

ESTHER   Well, I call it unnatural, and if I were Marjorie I
wouldn't give it house room.

MARY   (*busy eating*) What else have you had?

GEORGE   A couple of shirts from your mother and an instrument
of torture from Esther.

ESTHER   It's a chest expander and not before time. You're getting
flabby.
(MARJORIE *re-enters from the hall with a parcel and
several birthday cards. She stands between* GEORGE *and*
MARY.)

GEORGE   Next thing people will start kicking sand into my eyes.
Oh yes, and Mrs. Trudge gave me a blancmange.

MARJORIE   Actually it was her own recipe for Instant Whip.

GEORGE   Beautifully wrapped too.

MARY   Daddy!

MARJORIE   (*handing him the parcel and cards*) Here's something else and some cards. (*She kisses* MARY.) Good morning, darling.

MARY   'Morning, mummy.

GEORGE   (*unwrapping the parcel*) It's from Ben.

            (MARJORIE *picks up her tea and goes to sit on the sofa.*)

ESTHER   Oh, him!

GEORGE   Here we are again! (*He holds up a pair of grubby combinations.*)

MARJORIE   Oh no, not again!

MARY   Whatever is it?

GEORGE   Uncle Ben and I have been sending this pair of longjohns to one another every birthday for the last ten years.

            (MARJORIE *rises and picks up a letter which has fallen out of the parcel.*)

            They're looking a bit grubby. We shall have to give them a scrub one of these birthdays.

ESTHER   I can't think why you bother with him. He's a disgrace to the family.

GEORGE   Oh come now, Esther. Ben's not as bad as all that.

MARJORIE   (*reading the letter*) Oh dear!

GEORGE   What's the matter? What's he have to say?

MARJORIE   He's coming to stay.

GEORGE   (*jumping to his feet*) Oh no! Ooh no! I will not have that old reprobate in my house.

ESTHER   (*triumphantly*) There you are—the dark stranger! Doctor Cosmos never lies!

MARY   Goody for him.

GEORGE   Uncle Ben is no stranger—worse luck. And if he's dark it's probably dirt. And he is not coming here to stay!

MARJORIE   But George——

MARY   But Daddy, I've always been away at school when he's been before. I'm looking forward to meeting him!

GEORGE   No! Last time he filled my laboratory with tobacco plants and completely wrecked one of my most promising experiments. And then there was that business in church. I had to apologise to the vicar and resign from the golf club. He is not coming and that is final. Ugh! (*He thumps his fist on the table but rather spoils*

*the effect by landing on the remnants of the kipper. The
telephone rings and* GEORGE *stamps U.R. to answer it,
wagging his hand crossly. He speaks into phone.)*
Hallo?
(FRED *gives a loud buzz and coughs into life.)*

FRED   Hallo.

GEORGE   Hallo? Who's that?

FRED   This is a recorded statement.

GEORGE   *(waving his hand at* FRED*)* Who?

FRED   A recorded statement.

GEORGE   *(to* FRED*)* Ssh! *(Into phone.)* No, not you. I was talking
to the computer.— What?— Speak up. I can't hear you.

FRED   *(loudly)* This is a recorded statement. Mr. Shaw is out.

GEORGE   *(bellowing into phone)* This is Mr. Shaw.

FRED   One inch of rain on the surface of an acre weighs over
one hundred tons.

GEORGE   What? Oh lord! *(He puts down the phone, switches*
FRED *off and returns.)* Now then, what were you saying
about rain?— You didn't? Oh! Yes, yes. This is George
Shaw. Who's that?— Buller?— Oh, Puller.
(MARY *reacts at the name.)*
The advertisement? What advertisement?— Oh, that
one.— You did? *(His tone changes completely.)* Well
now, why don't you come round?
(He continues to talk quietly into the phone.)

MARJORIE   *(crossing below table)* Would you like a kipper, dear?

MARY   No, thanks. *(She is anxiously trying to listen to* GEORGE's
conversation.)

MARJORIE   How about some toast? You really ought to eat something.

MARY   *(craning her neck)* No mummy, really. I don't want a
thing.

ESTHER   Fresh fruit's the only thing. Have a banana.
(MARY *shakes her head, rises, and creeps towards*
GEORGE.)

MARJORIE   *(loading breakfast things on to the tray)* I wonder you
keep fit, Esther. All that fruit.

ESTHER   Ah. An apple a day keeps the doctor away.

MARJORIE   *(indicating the bowl of fruit)* Yes, but you don't have
to barricade the door with it.

ESTHER Doctor Cosmos forbids the relishing of dead flesh.

MARJORIE Oh, don't be horrid!

GEORGE (*finishing his conversation loudly*) You will? Good. Excellent. This morning then. Goodbye.
(*He puts down the phone and turns to find* MARY *close behind him.*)
There now. (*He comes across to C., rubbing his hands.*)

MARY Who was it?

GEORGE A young man called Puller. Nice young chap by the sound of him. He saw my advertisement and wants the job. He's coming round.

MARJORIE What about Miss Blossom?

GEORGE Who?

MARJORIE Miss Blossom—the girl who came round last night. (*She points at the french window.*) Didn't you ask her to call again today?

GEORGE Did I? Oh dash! So I did. I'd forgotten about her.

MARJORIE Well, it looks as though you're going to have to choose between her and this young fellow on the phone.
(*She goes to the kitchen with a loaded tray.*)

GEORGE Puller eh? Sounds foreign.

MARY (*crossing to* GEORGE) You did say his name was Puller?
(MRS. TRUDGE *enters from the kitchen dressed as in Act One but without her hat. She crosses to the stairs, carrying a lavatory brush and a tin of cleaner.*)

GEORGE Yes, why?

MRS. TRUDGE (*to no one in particular*) I'm going to clean round the bend. (*She goes upstairs.*)

MARY Did he mention me?

GEORGE Who, Mr. Puller? No. Why should he?

MARY I thought that was the whole idea—to find me a suitable mate.

MARJORIE (*entering from the kitchen*) Don't be primitive, Mary, it doesn't suit you. Where's Mrs. Trudge?

GEORGE She's gone clean round the bend. I must get to work. (*He picks up the white coat from the back of the sofa and starts to put it on.*) By the way, what's become of that other young fellow—Mr. Shorter? The one you made out was your young man.

MARY (*coming D.C.: crossly*) Once and for all he is not my

young man. I keep telling you I never saw him before yesterday.

GEORGE I don't hold with these short engagements.

ESTHER (*looking up from her magazine*) He's upstairs.

GEORGE Upstairs? What's he doing up there?

ESTHER Meditating.

GEORGE Does he have to do it in our house? Don't they have special places for that sort of thing?

MARJORIE You asked him to stay.

GEORGE Did I?

MARJORIE (*packing the remaining breakfast things on to the tray*) Yes, don't you remember? What with one thing and another last night he got all worked up and we had to give him a cup of cocoa to soothe him down and then he missed his last bus. He's up in the spare room.

GEORGE Doesn't he want any breakfast?

ESTHER He is searching for the truth.

(*There is a scream from upstairs and the sound of heavy footsteps.*)

MARY It sounds as though he's found it.

(MRS. TRUDGE *appears on the stairs, one hand pressed to her ample bosom.*)

MRS. TRUDGE Oh my Gawd!

MARY (*going to her aid and leading her* D.C.) Whatever's the matter, Mrs. T.?

MRS. TRUDGE There's a man standing on 'is 'ead in the bedroom!

ESTHER (*standing up*) Ah! Yogi!

MRS. TRUDGE I couldn't rightly say, not that way up. 'E 'asn't got a stitch on.

GEORGE Yogi bare.

MRS. TRUDGE Upset me, that 'as. I think I'm in for one of me turns. (*She looks hopefully at* GEORGE.) You 'aven't got a drop of something, I s'pose?

GEORGE No, I haven't. Last time you had one of your turns you polished off half a bottle of Scotch and went round singing 'Rule Britannia'.

MRS. TRUDGE Well, it's me nerves, you see.

GEORGE Oh, you've got a nerve all right.

ESTHER (*going to sideboard*) Come along now. Pull yourself together. Try some fruit juice.

MARJORIE (*crossing to* C.) Yes, Mrs. Trudge, you know how we rely on you.

MRS. TRUDGE Well, don't try me too 'ard. Bare-faced liars is one thing but when it comes to the naked truth, well——

ESTHER I hope you didn't interfere with his cogitations.

MRS. TRUDGE I never got near enough, don't you worry.

MARJORIE Why don't you come and make yourself a nice cup of tea?

MARY Yes, come along, Mrs. T. I'll give you a hand with the washing up.

(*They cosset her gently towards the kitchen.*)

MRS. TRUDGE Oh, that'll be a treat I'm sure. (*She points accusingly at* GEORGE.) 'Tis 'im and 'is computering! It ain't natural.

MARJORIE (*picking up the loaded tray and thrusting it into* MRS. TRUDGE'*s reluctant hands*) Yes, yes. Come along.

MRS. TRUDGE (*muttering to herself*) Next thing we shall be 'aving sparks coming out of the loo again.

(MARY, MRS. TRUDGE *and* MARJORIE *go out to the kitchen.*)

GEORGE (*crossing to* C.) I firmly believe that woman would like to see the house burn down just to prove she was right about me.

ESTHER (*moving to stairs*) I hope Mr. Shorter is all right. It's bad for anyone to have their meditation cut off short.

GEORGE Oh, I expect he'll come to earth in a minute.

ESTHER Do you think I ought to go up and look?

GEORGE I shouldn't, it might prove fatal. But I mustn't hang about here all day. (*He moves towards the laboratory.*) Fred needs attention. (*He goes into lab.*)

ESTHER (*calling after him*) Don't forget to change his nappy! He treats it like a baby. Ah, what a lovely day!

(*She moves across L. and does deep-breathing exercises in front of the window.* ALBERT SHORTER *appears on the stairs. He is wearing a dressing gown several sizes too large for him. He takes a few hesitant steps into the room.*)

ALBERT Excuse me!

ESTHER (*whirling round*) Ah! (*She advances, arms outstretched.*)

ALBERT (*retreating* U.R. *nervously*) I hope I'm not intruding.

ESTHER My dear young man. Come in, come in. We were just talking about you. (*She takes his arm and leads him D.C.*)

ALBERT   I was doing my morning exercises and a lady came in.
I hope I didn't alarm her. My trousers seem to have
vanished.

ESTHER   Not a bit, not a bit. Now come and sit down. How are
you feeling this morning? (*She sits him down* L. *of
table.*)

ALBERT   A little stronger, I think. But my trousers——

ESTHER   Don't worry about your trousers. They're quite safe.
I'm looking after them.

ALBERT   I'm not used to all this excitement.

ESTHER   Of course not, but now tell me all about your transmigration.

ALBERT   Transmi—? Oh that.

ESTHER   Yes. My very first case. Isn't it thrilling? What was it
like?

ALBERT   I don't think I could face it, not without my trousers.

ESTHER   Come, come now, don't be modest. (*She crosses to the
sideboard.*) Have some fruit-juice.
(ALBERT *shakes his head.*)

ALBERT   No, thank you. Well—— (*He pauses.*)

ESTHER   Well?

ALBERT   No, I can't.

ESTHER   Then I shall withhold your trousers until you change
your mind.

ALBERT   (*jumping to his feet*) But you can't do that!

ESTHER   Oh, can't I? (*She advances and he shuffles back towards
the sofa.*) Mr. Shorter—Albert—I implore you—I com-
mand you! Tell me—everything! Sit down.
(*He does so, on the very edge of the sofa.*)
Now concentrate! Let everything slip out of your mind.
Relax! I said relax! (*She puts her hand on his forehead
and pushes him roughly back.*) You are going back, back,
back to the day it all started.
(ALBERT'S *eyes close.*)
You are going to sleep—sleep—sleep.
(ALBERT *snores loudly.*)
Not that far asleep!
(*She pokes him viciously and his eyes jerk open.*)
You're not trying!

ALBERT   I haven't had any breakfast.

ESTHER How can you think about food at a time like this?

ALBERT My tummy's rumbling so loud I can't hear what I'm thinking.

ESTHER Concentrate, young man.

ALBERT Perhaps if I had something to eat——

ESTHER Oh here! (*She takes a banana from the bowl on the table and thrusts it into his hand.*)

ALBERT Thanks. (*He starts to peel it.*)

ESTHER Now then, let's try again. And let yourself go this time.
(*And again she pushes him forcefully back into the sofa.*)
Back, back. You are going back. Back——
(*And indeed he does slide steadily up the back of the sofa until he suddenly disappears over the top.* ESTHER *picks him up and dusts him down. She thrusts the banana back into his hand and sits him down again.*)
You're not trying. Now then. Watch my finger!
(*She wags it to and fro like a metronome and* ALBERT'S *head begins to follow suit. His banana joins in but wags the opposite way.*)
You are going to sleep.
(MARY *comes in quietly from the kitchen and stands by the door fascinated.*)
Sleep—sleep—deep deep sleep.
Sleep—sleep—deep deep sleep.

MARY What's this, dancing lessons?
(ESTHER *throws up her hands in despair.*)

ESTHER Oh, it's hopeless! I might as well give up trying.

MARY (*moving to* C.) Sorry, auntie. I thought I heard something fall over. What's the matter with him?
(*They both stare at* ALBERT, *who has been struck like a statue, the banana half-raised to his lips.*)

ESTHER Mr. Shorter? Albert? (*She makes a pass in front of his face without effect.*) Good gracious, I've done it! He's gone off.

MARY He never did look very healthy.

ESTHER Well I never! It's never worked before. Isn't it exciting?

MARY He doesn't look wildly thrilled.

ESTHER I just made a pass at him and——

MARY No wonder he came over all of a doo-dah.

ESTHER (*striding round in great excitement*) But think what it means. The power. The influence. Why, your father will never dare be rude to me again.

MARY   (*looking closely at* ALBERT) Hadn't you better bring him round?

ESTHER   (*above sofa*) It seems such a waste. Couldn't I do something with him while he's under the influence?

MARY   It depends what you had in mind.

ESTHER   I mean couldn't I take advantage of the situation?

MARY   Better not. He's gone a bit green round the gills.

ESTHER   Oh dear. Well, in that case perhaps I'd better—— (*She shakes him by the shoulder without effect.*) Come along, there's a stout fellow. Wake up. Come along.

MARY   Mr. Shorter. (*Loudly in his ear.*) Mr. Shorter! It's no use, he's well away.

ESTHER   Oh bother. I can't remember how to bring him round. I've never had to do it before. It's really very thoughtless of him. I believe he's doing it to provoke me. (*She moves* U.C.)

MARY   Well, you can't leave him like that.

ESTHER   (*considering* ALBERT *with her head on one side*) Oh, I don't know. He's rather decorative.

MARY   Yes, something like a Picasso. Anyway Mrs. Trudge would never put up with dusting him every day.

ESTHER   (*moving to the stairs*) No, I suppose you're right. Just keep an eye on him for a moment, there's a good girl.

MARY   (*moving up to* ESTHER *in alarm*) Where are you going?

ESTHER   I'm going to look it up in my books. I might have known things would go wrong today. Mondays are always difficult. (*She mounts the bottom stair.*)

MARY   But it's Tuesday.

ESTHER   (*turning*) Well, there you are, you see.
    (*She goes upstairs and* MARY *goes to the foot of the stairs and calls up.*)

MARY   And don't be long. It's like being shut up with a zombie!
    (*She returns to the sofa and reaches out at arm's length to pick up a magazine from beside* ALBERT, *who sits unmoving. She crosses and sits L. of table and after a further glance at him starts to read, sitting on the edge of her chair. Suddenly* FRED *speaks.*)

FRED   Good morning!

(MARY *screams and throws the magazine into the air.*
She jumps to her feet to face FRED.)

We will now sing Hymn No. 61—'Christians awake!'
(GEORGE *enters from the laboratory*.)

GEORGE That's got it working again. A spot of fluff on his syn-
dicator. Lend me a hand, will you, Mary? I want to try
out a new experiment.

MARY (*pointing at* ALBERT) I'm keeping an eye on him.

GEORGE Why, what's he up to?

MARY Nothing. That's just the trouble. I think his elastic's
broken.

GEORGE Oh, never mind him. He's probably meditating again.
He won't even notice you've gone. Come along.
(MARY *goes into lab and* GEORGE *follows after a sorrow-*
ful shake of the head at ALBERT.

No sooner have they gone than ALBERT *comes to life.*
He puts the banana down and tries to peep through the
keyhole. Then he takes out a notebook from his dressing-
gown pocket, stands in front of the machine and starts
to make a sketch of it. FRED *suddenly buzzes to life.*)

FRED Pheasant shooting starts on the second of October.
(ALBERT *jumps. The front door bell rings. He stuffs his*
book away and freezes into a statuesque attitude beside
FRED.)
Buchan's cold spell ninth to fourteenth May.

ALBERT Ssh! Somebody's coming.

FRED The eight-forty-five train for Turnham Green will leave
from Platform Three.

ALBERT Yes, yes. Now be quiet.
(*He resumes his imitation of the Venus de Milo as* MRS.
TRUDGE *enters from the kitchen. She limps across in*
front of him, apparently unaware of his presence. He
follows her with his eyes.)

FRED Tickets please!
(MRS. TRUDGE *turns and* ALBERT'S *eyes snap to the front.*)

MRS. TRUDGE Yogi! Hmph!
(*She goes out to the hall.* ALBERT *takes out his note-book*
again and resumes his sketching, using the banana to
measure the perspective. Edging slowly backwards with
the banana at arm's length he collides with the arm of

*the sofa and falls backwards to resume his old position
on the sofa just as* MRS. TRUDGE *re-enters from the hall
followed by* UNCLE BEN. BEN *is a mischievous extrovert
a few years younger than* GEORGE. *The sort of man every
boy would like his uncle to be and who must be hell to
live with. He is dressed in a flashy sports jacket and is
wearing a flat cap at a jaunty angle.*)

MRS. TRUDGE In 'ere. 'Oo did you say you were?

BEN (*moving to C. and surveying the room*) Parker's the
name, Ben Parker. You'll have heard about me from
Marj.

MRS. TRUDGE (*on her dignity*) If you mean Mrs. Shaw I don't concern
myself with the family's business.

BEN You mean to say you haven't heard of Uncle Ben?

MRS. TRUDGE Oh you're 'im, are you? I'll tell Mr. Shaw you're 'ere.
(*She moves towards the laboratory.*)

BEN (*hurriedly taking her arm*) I wouldn't worry the old
fellow. Not yet awhile. Got to give him a chance to pre-
pare for the shock.

MRS. TRUDGE Oh, 'e's expecting you, don't you fret.

BEN Oh, he knows I'm coming, does he? (*He leads her D.C.*)
What did he say? Glad to be seeing me again, eh?

MRS. TRUDGE 'E said 'e was ready for you. Give us yer 'at.

BEN It wouldn't match your jumper.

MRS. TRUDGE Suit yerself. I always says you can tell a gentleman by
'is manners. (*She stumps towards the kitchen.*)

BEN That's all right then. I suppose you're old mother Trudge.
(*He follows her across.*)

MRS. TRUDGE I'll thank you to keep a civil tongue in yer 'ead!
(BEN *smacks her on the bottom.*)

BEN That's what I like to hear I like a woman with a bit of
spirit.

MRS. TRUDGE (*hobbling smartly above the table*) You keep yer 'ands
to yerself. I'm sure I don't know what Mr. Shaw's going
to say about this. (*She marches to the lab door.*)

BEN I do. He'll start tut-tutting all over the place like an out-
board motor. But you're not going to tell me a handsome
woman like you takes exception to a friendly gesture.

MRS. TRUDGE (*pausing by the lab door*) Is that what you call it? Well,
I ain't used to that sort of thing.

BEN   You mean to say George doesn't get you in a dark corner now and again?

MRS. TRUDGE   I should think not indeed!

BEN   He must be slipping. Regular one for the girls is George. You'll have to watch him. (*In a hoarse whisper.*) Particularly when he's all alone in the lab.

(MRS. TRUDGE *edges away from the lab door.*)

MRS. TRUDGE   Yus. Well, on second thoughts I'll tell Mrs. Shaw first. (*She goes into kitchen.* BEN *walks round* ALBERT, *who sits unflinching. He wags his hand up and down in front of* ALBERT's *face without result. He then transfers his cap to* ALBERT's *head, takes out a large pipe and matches, turns up one of* ALBERT's *slippered feet, strikes a match on it and lights his pipe. He turns away to examine* FRED *and* ALBERT *at last moves his head to watch.* BEN *turns back and* ALBERT *clicks to eyes-front just in time. This happens again but this time* BEN *catches him looking.*)

BEN   Aha! Caught you. What is it, a sort of game?

ALBERT   Ssh!

BEN   Oh, you can talk too, can you?

(*He comes close and puffs smoke into* ALBERT'S *face.* ALBERT *coughs and waves it away.*)

ALBERT   Grrugh! What on earth are you smoking?

BEN   (*admiring his pipe*) Home-grown. Do you like it?

ALBERT   No. It smells like boiled boots.

BEN   Ah. That'll be the curing. I soak it in Friar's Balsam.

ALBERT   Well, I don't want to worry you but that friar must have had something wrong with his balsam.

BEN   You don't look too good yourself. What are you playing at? (*He sits down next to* ALBERT.)

ALBERT   Ssh! I'm in trouble.

BEN   Get away! You don't look strong enough.

ALBERT   (*indicating upstairs*) It's her.

BEN   Who? Mrs. Trudge?

ALBERT   No, the one with the ramparts.

BEN   You must mean Esther. She's a bit old to be in trouble, isn't she?

ALBERT   She thinks she's put me into a trance.

BEN   You could have fooled me too. It's the first time Esther's entranced anyone in her life.

ALBERT But what am I going to do? You won't tell her, will
you?

BEN Depends what you're up to, me old dear. We can't have
people lying around the place pretending to be sent.

ALBERT Oh dear, I'm not supposed to say. If I tell you will you
promise not to give me away?

BEN All right. I won't give you away if you help me to
quieten old George down if he gets excited. (*He listens
at the lab door.*) What's he doing in there, I wonder?

ALBERT I think he said he was having trouble with a bit of fluff.

BEN Is he, the old rascal? Look out!

(ALBERT *freezes back into his old position as* MARJORIE
enters from the kitchen.)

MARJORIE Ben!

(*He comes* D.C. *and holds out his arms. She runs to him
and they embrace in a friendly way.*)

BEN Watcher, Marj, me old beauty. Glad to see me? Let's
have a look at you. (*He holds her at arm's length.*)
Haven't changed a bit. I don't know how you manage
it.

MARJORIE Oh, get away with you! It's years since you've been
here.

BEN And whose fault is that?

MARJORIE Oh yes, I know. But George——
(*She suddenly catches sight of* ALBERT.)
Oh, Mr. Shorter. I didn't see you there. Are you feeling
better? (*She crosses and looks closely at him.*) Is he all
right, do you think?

BEN Right as ninepence. He's under the influence.

MARJORIE At this time in the morning?

BEN Shocking, isn't it? Take no notice, he may go away.

MARJORIE Don't you think I ought to get him something?

BEN Like what—a blood transfusion? Don't you bother,
Esther's looking after him. Did you get my letter?

MARJORIE Yes, it arrived with the long-johns—I mean George's
present.

BEN I thought I'd better give you a bit of warning after so
long.

MARJORIE Yes, all of half an hour. Thanks!

BEN It'll be all right for a day or two, won't it?

MARJORIE Well, it's George.

BEN He doesn't take up all that much room, surely? Oh don't tell me he's still sore about what happened last time. *(He walks to the sideboard.)*

MARJORIE Well, you were rather naughty.

BEN What, putting a banger on the lavatory chain?

MARJORIE No, it wasn't that. It was the rude cushions in the church pews. He's never got over that.

BEN *(picking up the clock-works)* That woke 'em up a bit! Right in the middle of New Every Morning. It still rankles, eh?

MARJORIE Yes, he says he won't have you in the house at any price.

BEN Silly old scientist. *(He puts down the clock-works.)* What about you?

MARJORIE Oh yes, he puts up with me.

BEN *(crossing to her)* No. I mean will you let me stay?

MARJORIE Oh dear. I know it's going to mean trouble.

BEN It's either here or the haystack.

MARJORIE Well, you can't stay in a haystack. You'd set it on fire in five minutes. But I'm not sure about the room.

BEN *(to sofa)* Don't worry about that. I can share with Roger the lodger here. He won't mind. Will you, matey? *(He smacks ALBERT on the back. ALBERT grimaces.)*

MARJORIE Oh, all right then. But I know I'll regret it. *(She moves D.R.)* Only for goodness' sake keep out of George's way until I've broken the news to him gently.

GEORGE *(off)* Marjorie! Can you spare a minute?

MARJORIE *(calling)* Coming, dear! *(She goes to the lab door.)* By the way, I don't know what you've been saying to Mrs. Trudge about George but she refuses to go near him. *(MARJORIE goes to lab and BEN goes to the sideboard and pours himself a stiff whisky.)*

BEN Want one?

ALBERT No, thank you. *(He lowers the banana but stays looking straight ahead.)*

BEN Please yourself. What's up? Have you got stuck again?

ALBERT Did you have to say I was under the influence? I'm TT.

BEN Never mind. You'll grow out of it. Cheers! *(He drinks down his whisky at a gulp and pours himself another.)*

I'm glad Marj said I could stay. I've already asked the station to send my stuff up by taxi.

ALBERT   Don't you think you've had enough of that for one day?

BEN   What? Miss out on the Freemans? Not likely. George shouldn't leave the stuff lying about to tempt people. (*He picks up* ESTHER's *bottle of fruit juice.*) Hallo, what's this? (*Reads.*) 'Bobbo Pure Fruit Juice for Clean Living'! Ugh! That'll be Esther's or I'm an elephant. Let's see if we can't brighten her life for her.

ALBERT   What are you doing?

(BEN *pours half the bottle of Scotch into the remains of the fruit juice and shakes it up well.*)

BEN   There now. That'll put whiskers on her chin.

ALBERT   I shall inform Mrs. Shaw.

BEN   Oh, will you now? And I thought you were the one who wanted me to keep my mouth shut.

ALBERT   Oh dear, I wish I'd never come.

BEN   (*sitting* L. *of table*) Well, why did you come? To have your bumps read?

ALBERT   No, that was just an excuse to get into the house. (*He rises and moves* D.L.) I suppose you wouldn't like to earn—er—five pounds?

BEN   Depends what I had to do. If it's work, you're talking to the wrong chicken.

ALBERT   No, nothing like that. I want you to find out the truth about Mr. Shaw's digital prognosticator.

BEN   Oh, is that all! And what the devil is a digital prog-wotsit?

ALBERT   (*pointing to* FRED) That is.

BEN   (*turning to look*) Oh it is, is it? I thought it was a do-it-yourself Bingo outfit.

ALBERT   And if it can do what he claims it can it's worth a lot of money.

BEN   (*going up and stroking it*) We-ell now.

ALBERT   (*stepping forward*) Careful!

(BEN *snatches his hand away.*)

BEN   What does it do—bite?

ALBERT   No, it tells fortunes.

BEN   My old grandma used to do that and she finished up with a sink full of tea-leaves.

ALBERT Ah, but she didn't always get it right.

BEN And you're trying to tell me this does?

ALBERT Yes.

BEN (*after another look at* FRED) Pull the other one, it plays tunes.

ALBERT (*moving D.L. and taking a wallet out of his dressing-gown pocket*) My—er—colleagues have reason to believe it does. And they are willing to pay a small sum to find out for certain.

BEN (*moving eagerly down to* ALBERT) How much?

ALBERT Five pounds.
     (BEN *turns away in disgust.*)
     Ten pounds?

BEN Don't bust yourself.

ALBERT (*a little anxiously*) Twenty?

BEN Getting warmer.

FRED Twenty-five.

ALBERT What?

BEN Thirty.

ALBERT (*putting the wallet away again*) Cash on delivery.

BEN Bingo!
     (FRED *strikes one and delivers his invisible jackpot again.* BEN *goes to shake hands but seizes the banana by mistake and throws it on the floor.*)

ALBERT You understand this is a rather delicate matter? (*He sits L. of table.*)

BEN For thirty quid I can balance on a blancmange. What do you want me to do?

ALBERT I want you to test the machine.

BEN Yes, but how?

ALBERT Take this list of questions, (*He draws a piece of paper out from his wallet.*) and get the computer to give you the answers.

BEN (*taking the piece of paper*) And just how do I do that?

ALBERT I suggest you—Ssh! Somebody's coming. Quick, hide!

BEN (*pointing to the cupboard under the stairs*) What's in there?

ALBERT I wouldn't recommend that——
     (*But by this time* BEN *is peering in.*)

BEN Oh, this'll do. (*He disappears into the cupboard and his head emerges.*) Thirty quid, don't forget.

ALBERT Cash on delivery. (*He takes up his original position on the sofa but realising he hasn't got his banana he jumps to his feet.*) Banana! banana! Where's the banana!

FRED On the floor!

ALBERT Thanks!

(ALBERT *retrieves his fruit and returns to his old place on the sofa.* BEN *shuts the cupboard door.* ESTHER *comes slowly down the stairs, thumbing through a book.*)

ESTHER (*reading*) Necromancy—Geomancy—Little of what you Fancy! That's no good. What's this? Build your own oracle with Bodes and Augurs—that must be the carpentry section. Reading the entrails of a black cock! Good gracious, I don't think we've got one. I wonder if a budgerigar would do? (*She throws up her hands in despair.*) Not a thing about trances. I've looked everywhere. (*She peers round over her spectacles.*) Where have you got to, Mary? (*She comes downstairs and looks into* ALBERT'S *face.*) How are you feeling? (*She speaks slowly and loudly as to a young child.*) Can—you—hear—me? (*She sniffs at him suspiciously.*) There is a distinct smell of burning in this room. You haven't got a temperature, I suppose? (*She puts her hand on his forehead.*) Extraordinary! I wonder if—wait a minute. (*She crosses to the sideboard and rummages in a drawer.*) I know I put it somewhere. Ah, yes, here we are. (*She takes out a large pack-needle on a thread.* ALBERT, *who has been watching this out of the corner of his eye, reacts unfavourably.*) This should do the trick!

(*She advances on* ALBERT *flourishing the needle. He tries to watch what she is up to without actually turning his head.*)

Now then——

(*She stands behind him, needle poised, and* ALBERT'S *head tries to shrink into his collar in anticipation of a sudden jab. But* ESTHER *dangles the needle over his head on the end of the thread.*)

Let me see now. Side to side male; round and round female.

(*The needle swings round in an extravagant circle and* ALBERT *looks up at it in some annoyance.*)
Hmm! Most unusual!
(*She stands for a moment tapping the needle against his arm while* ALBERT *looks anxiously at it out of the corner of his eye.* FRED *breaks into life.*)

FRED Three pounds four and eightpence ha'penny.

ESTHER What?
(*She whirls round to look at* FRED *and stabs* ALBERT *in the arm.*)

ALBERT Eek!
(*He jumps up and down, holding his arm.* MARY *comes running in from the laboratory.*)

MARY Auntie!

ALBERT I've been stabbed!

ESTHER (*coming D.C. and waving the needle about*) Nonsense! It's only a little needle.

MARY Are you all right, Mr. Shorter?

ALBERT Oh, don't worry about me. I'm just quietly bleeding to death.

ESTHER Don't exaggerate, young man. It's nothing to make a fuss about. Anyway it brought you round, that's the main thing.

ALBERT Thanks very much! (*He ties himself into a knot trying to examine his wound.*)

ESTHER (*taking his arm*) Now I think you ought to go and lie down for a while to recover.

ALBERT But I don't want to lie down! I just want to go home! (*He is almost in tears.*) I wish I'd never come.

ESTHER Now, now. You're overwrought. Take his other arm, Mary.
(MARY *crosses and takes* ALBERT'S *arm.*)
You have a nice quiet lie down and you'll soon feel better.
(*They steer him protesting towards the stairs.*)

ALBERT I want my trousers.

ESTHER (*soothing*) Yes, yes. All in good time. Just come upstairs and let me put some herbs on that little pinprick.

ALBERT (*petulantly*) It's not a little pinprick. It's a bloody great hole!

ESTHER Now, now! That's quite enough of that. We don't want to have our mouths washed out, do we? (*She darts across to the sideboard and picks up the bottle of 'laced' fruit juice.*) We'd better take up some nice fruit juice to drink. So much nicer than that horrid whisky.

ALBERT No, no! Anything but the fruit juice!

ESTHER Up we go. That's the way!
(*And they disappear round the bend of the stairs with* ALBERT *in tow. The front door bell rings and* BEN *emerges from the cupboard and shouts.*)

BEN Mrs. Trudge! Shop! (*He digs out of his pocket the piece of paper* ALBERT *has given him.*) Now then, let's have a look at these questions.
(MRS. TRUDGE *enters from the kitchen and crosses to hall.*)

MRS. TRUDGE You still 'ere?

BEN Oh, you won't get rid of me in a hurry.

MRS. TRUDGE Hm! We'll see about that. (*She goes out to hall.*)

BEN Happy, smiling faces! Now then, let's see—(*He comes D.C., reading.*) 'Three-quarters of a pound chuck steak, eight pounds King Edwards. A packet of frozen peas!' What on earth! (*He turns the paper over.*) Ah! This is more like it. 'Newmarket two-thirty, four-thirty Lingfield Park'—don't tell me Albert's playing the horses. Ben, Ben, you're on to something.
(MRS. TRUDGE *returns with* PETER, *who is wearing a red wig and horn-rimmed spectacles. Not a becoming outfit.*)

PETER (*speaking with a strong French accent*) I am ringing up about zis advertisement and he is saying come round so I am coming.

MRS. TRUDGE Well, you can stop coming now, 'cause you're 'ere. What do you want?

PETER Not vot—'oo?

MRS. TRUDGE And 'oo to you too! If you're selling something we don't want any and if you've come round about the Common Market we always get our stuff at the grocer's down in the village. (*To* BEN.) I can't make out what 'e's on about.

PETER (*to* BEN) I am vishing to see Mr. Shaw.

BEN (*to* MRS. TRUDGE) He vishes to see Mr. Shaw.

MRS. TRUDGE Well, why don't 'e say so then instead of vishing and
voshing all over the place like one of them soap adverts.
I'll give 'im a shout. (*She goes to the lab door but stops
short.*) No, I won't. 'E might get up to something in
there. You'd better wait 'ere till he comes out. (*She
limps to the kitchen door.*) I dunno why you foreigners
can't stop in your own place. Coming over 'ere selling
people onions. It's all this migration—I don't 'old with
it! (*She goes to the kitchen.*)
(PETER *makes a Gallic gesture to* BEN.)

BEN Don't mind her. She's not herself today. The name's Ben
—Ben Parker.
(PETER *crosses to C. and they shake hands.* PETER
*attempts to click his heels but only succeeds in cracking
his ankle bones together.*)

PETER Peter—ouch! I mean Pierre Poulleur—from Paris—in
France! 'Ow do you do?

BEN Come to see George—Mr. Shaw?

PETER Yes. I mean *oui*! I am French.

BEN Yes, you would be, coming from France. You're not
after it too, are you?

PETER It?

BEN George's computer.

PETER Oh no! I am after something else.
(MARY *enters down the stairs, stops short at seeing* PETER
and runs into his arms.)

MARY Peter! Darling!
(*They kiss passionately and* PETER *loses his wig. He looks
up at* BEN *over* MARY's *shoulder and gives another Gallic
shrug.*)

BEN Yes, I see what you mean. I always reckoned the French
were a bit quick off the mark!
(*He saunters round the engrossed pair and picks up the
wig.* PETER *starts to stroke* MARY's *seat. After a couple
of passes* FRED *coughs into action.*)

FRED At the third stroke it will be——

BEN Too late! (*He taps* PETER *on the shoulder and hands him
his wig.*)
You seem to have blown your top!

PETER (*emerging momentarily*) Thanks very much!

(*He returns to his kiss.* BEN *coughs loudly.* PETER *and* MARY *reluctantly unwrap and* PETER *puts the wig back on again.*)

BEN   Let me introduce myself. I'm your Uncle Ben. And this is Pierre Poulleur from Paris.

MARY   No, it isn't. It's Peter Puller from Penge. We're going to be married. Oh, do take off that dreadful wig. It makes you look like a chrysanthemum. What's the idea?

PETER   It's a disguise. I've come in answer to the advert.

MARY   You? But you don't know anything about computers.

PETER   Oh I don't know. I was pretty good at vulgar fractions at school.

BEN   I used to be an expert at rude stories.

PETER   I thought if I could twist Fred about a bit I might persuade him to change his mind.

MARY   About us? Oh darling, would you do that for me?

BEN   Romantic, isn't it?

MARY   You won't give us away, will you, Uncle Ben?

BEN   (*sauntering D.L. and perching on the sofa arm*) Not me. But that French accent of yours will.

PETER   I thought it was pretty good.

BEN   It's awful! Just you stick to English. George'll never notice the difference.
(*The doorbell rings.*)

MARY   We are doing a roaring trade today. (*She calls to the kitchen.*) All right, Mrs. Trudge. I'll get it. (*To* BEN.) She's not herself today. (*To* PETER.) Excuse me, darling. (*She goes out to hall.*)

BEN   You've got a good lass there.

PETER   (*coming D.C.*) Yes, if I can persuade Mr. Shaw to take it as red. (*He points to his head.*)

BEN   When you find out how that gadget works, (*He points at* FRED.) you might tip me the wink. I've got a bit of business to transact.
(*He waves his piece of paper around and pops it in his pocket.* MARY *enters from the hall with* POPPY.)

MARY   (*a trifle sharply*) If you would care to wait in here, Miss Blossom, I'll tell my father you've called. Oh, you haven't met my uncle and Mr.—er—Puller. Miss Blossom. (*She crosses to lab door.*)

BEN (*waving his pipe*) How do!

PETER Good morning.

POPPY Good heavens!

MARY Miss Blossom is here in answer to the advertisement.

PETER Oh lord!

(MARY *gives him a hard look and goes out to lab.*)

BEN (*moving across in front of sofa and* U.C.) This is where I make myself scarce before George turns up and thinks I'm after the job too. (*To* PETER.) Let me know when the coast's clear.

(*He goes into the cupboard and shuts the door.* POPPY *goes and inspects the door and looks enquiringly at* PETER.)

POPPY Does he live in there?

PETER Only during the day. He hangs from the picture rail at night. Better not mention him, they don't like to talk about it! You've come about the advert. then.

POPPY Yes.

PETER So have I.

POPPY Bad luck!

PETER What? Oh yes—a bit of competition. Er—do you know about computers as well then?

POPPY As well as what?

PETER As well as all your other unfair advantages?

POPPY Yes.

PETER Oh!

POPPY Do you?

PETER No—I mean yes! (*A pause.*) Not much point in us both waiting, is there?

POPPY (*sitting firmly on the sofa*) No!

PETER Er—no!

(*He has been fiddling with the knobs on* FRED *who bursts into full voice.*)

FRED Fifteen stone four pounds.

(PETER *switches it off again and backs* D.C.)

PETER Fascinating, isn't it?

POPPY (*rising and crossing to* PETER) All right. Where is it?

PETER Eh? Oh. Second on the right outside. (*He points.*)

POPPY I'm talking about the secret plans.

PETER Plans? Plans? What plans?

POPPY The plans of the computer.

PETER How should I know?

POPPY You can't fool me. I know a disguise when I see one. Let's stop beating about the bush. I don't know who you are but it's obvious we're both after the same thing.

PETER I hope not.

POPPY (*coming up close to* PETER) Why don't we pool resources?

PETER Here, I say, you're steaming up my glasses. (*He takes them off and rubs them with a hanky, pulling it through the frames to emphasise the fact that there are no lenses.*) I don't know what you're talking about.

POPPY There's no need to pretend with me. You want the secret of that thing and so do I. (*She smooches up close again.*) Let's get together!

(PETER *puts his glasses back on and looks at her over the top of them.* GEORGE *suddenly enters from the lab and* PETER *takes refuge behind* POPPY *and above the sofa.* GEORGE *is still wearing his white coat and is carrying a large screw-driver.* MARY *follows close behind.*)

GEORGE Sorry to keep you. I had a screw loose. Now then, let's see—which one is Miss Blossom?

POPPY (*advancing seductively, hand outstretched*) Good morning, Mr. Shaw. You asked me to come round this morning.

GEORGE (*shaking hands*) Er—yes. How do you do?

PETER (*from behind* POPPY) And I'm Peter Puller. (*He tries to shake hands but* POPPY *keeps getting in the way.*)

GEORGE That rings a bell.

PETER Only if it's a bell-puller. (*He is delighted at this joke which* GEORGE *doesn't appreciate.*)

MARY (*hurriedly*) Oh, it's a very common name, isn't it, Mr. Puller?

PETER Oh yes, very.

GEORGE Oh yes, now I remember. You were the young man who telephoned. And now you've both come about the advertisement Most gratifying—but a little awkward because I only have the one position to offer——

MARY (*quickly*) And we were after a man.

POPPY (*aside*) Aren't we all?

GEORGE Well, I must admit I did have a male assistant in mind.

POPPY (*digging in her handbag*) What, with this description? (*She reads from a newspaper cutting.*) 'Red hair and good figure-work essential.' There's nothing wrong with my figure-work. (*She parades around to prove it.*)

PETER By george! Yes, I see what you mean. Well, I suppose in that case I shall have to—Ow! Ooh!
(MARY *has kicked him on the shin. She propels him forward into the limelight.*)

MARY Peter—I mean Mr. Puller is very well qualified, aren't you, darling? I mean doctor?

GEORGE Doctor?

PETER Eh? Oh yes. First class honours in—er—long division.

MARY And besides, daddy, I could hardly marry Miss Blossom, could I? Mr. Puller looks just about right to me.

GEORGE Yes, yes, quite right. Well then, young lady, I'm afraid——

POPPY (*taking out documents from her bag*) Certificate of Advanced Technology, Testimonial of Applied Binaries and—Duxford's Digital Diploma!

GEORGE (*greatly impressed*) Duxford's Digital Diploma?

POPPY With honours.

GEORGE (*shaking her hand eagerly*) My dear young lady. I'm proud to have you in the house. Duxford's Digital Diploma. My gracious me!

MARY (*to* PETER) Well, don't just stand there. Do something or she'll get the job.

PETER What can I do? It's that duck thing she's got. All I've got is a chicken-pox mark.

GEORGE (*going to* FRED) Let me give you a demonstration. Just stand on there.
(POPPY *stands on the step in front of* FRED.)

FRED Thirty-eight, twenty-four, thirty-six!
(*He gives a loud wolf-whistle.*)

GEORGE I think he's getting overheated. You must be standing too close.

FRED Grrr! Ruff! Ruff!
(POPPY *backs away in consternation.*)

GEORGE Hmm! High tension!

PETER Better put bromide in his oil.

GEORGE (to POPPY) Well, never mind. Come and sit down.
(POPPY *sits above table.*)
You'll find us a quiet family. No excitement. I always say excitement ruins the scientific approach.
(*From upstairs comes the sound of* ESTHER *singing* Nellie Dean.)

ESTHER (*off*) There's an old mill by the stream—Nellie Dean!

POPPY What's that?

MARY It sounds like Aunt Esther.

ESTHER (*off*) Where I used to sit and dream, Nellie Dean!

GEORGE Esther—singing?

PETER If you can call it that!

ESTHER (*off*) And the watersh ash they flow——
(*She rolls into sight round the bend in the stairs, her turban askew and the bottle of fruit-juice, now almost empty, in her hand.* GEORGE *moves across as though to catch her and she leans on him for support, beating time with the bottle.*)
Sheem to whishper shoft and low!
Yoou're my heart's desire, I looooves yer—Nellie Dean!
Hello, George—have shome fruit juish.

GEORGE Esther! What on earth is the matter with you?

ESTHER S'nothing the marrer with me. I jus' been havin' a lil' drink with my frien' Albert Shortpiece. (*She spots* POPPY *and comes* D.C.) Hallo! Who's the lil' lady, George? (*She sings.*) Hallo! Hallo! Who's your lady frien'? Who's the lil'—— (*Confidentially to* POPPY.) You wanna watchim. It's the lil' ones you gotta watch.

GEORGE Now, now, Esther, control yourself.

ESTHER (*spotting* PETER *in his wig*) Goo' lord! Wha's that? (*She inspects him closely.*) You're not Albert Shortshift. Wharrave you done with Albert? He's my bes' frien'. My very bes' frien'. (*She rolls to the stairs and calls.*) Albert!

ALBERT (*off*) I'm jus' coming.

ESTHER He's a bit shy 'cos he's lost his trousers.
(*She leans against the cupboard for support.* ALBERT *appears on the stairs wearing a singlet and jazzy striped*

underpants. He is carrying GEORGE's *chest expander. He staggers down the last few steps and into the room.*)

GEORGE		Good lord!
MARY	(*together*)	Look out!
PETER		My God!

ALBERT (*trying out the chest expander*) Anyone for tennis?
(*He falls flat on his back* C. *and* PETER *bends down and tries to revive him with an odd sort of artificial respiration.*)

ESTHER (*looking down beatifically*) Isn't he cute? He looks like a stick of rock.

GEORGE (*taking* ESTHER's *arm*) This is a fine display, I must say. Esther, go to your room.

ESTHER (*shaking him off*) And you go to h—have a drink. (*She pushes him aside and wanders a little unsteadily round the room to sit R. of table.*)
(*The front-door bell rings.*)

MARY Oh, not another one! I couldn't stand it.

PETER (*still flailing* ALBERT's *arms*) I can't bring him round.

POPPY Try the kiss of life.
(PETER *bends down towards* ALBERT *but catches a whiff of his breath and recoils hastily.*)

PETER Not likely, it'd kill me!

GEORGE (*gingerly coming behind* ESTHER's *chair*) Now, now, Esther. Everything's going to be all right. Mary, help me to get her upstairs.
(MARY *crosses to* C. ESTHER *stands up and brandishes the bottle at her.*)

ESTHER You keep off or I'll bop you with the bottle.
(MRS. TRUDGE *enters from the kitchen and stands directly behind* ESTHER.)

MRS. TRUDGE Excuse me, did I 'ear the bell?

ESTHER Seconds out!
(*She swings the bottle back over her shoulder and accidently hits* MRS. TRUDGE *over the head. That unfortunate lady subsides into the arms of* GEORGE *who happens to be standing there.*)

GEORGE My dear, good woman! Mary, quick, give me a hand. Her feather's tickling my nose.
(*The front-door bell rings again.*)

MARY What about the front door?

GEORGE Oh yes, yes, yes, all right! But hurry.
  (MARY *goes out to the hall.* GEORGE *appeals to* PETER.)
  Perhaps you wouldn't mind helping me——
  (PETER *jumps over* ALBERT *and runs across above table to help* GEORGE. *At once* ALBERT *sits upright.*)

PETER Loosen her collar.

ALBERT I'm going to be sick.

ESTHER Nonsense. It's all in the mind.

POPPY (*drawing her feet in*) Well, if we don't look out it'll all be on the carpet.
  (PETER *plucks the bowler-hat off the bust and puts it in a strategic position in front of* ALBERT. GEORGE *meanwhile is trying to loosen* MRS. TRUDGE's *collar.* MRS. TRUDGE *comes to herself again.*)

MRS. TRUDGE What 'appened? Where am I?

GEORGE There, there!

MRS. TRUDGE (*finding herself in* GEORGE's *arms, apparently being undressed*) 'Elp! 'Elp! 'E's got me. (*She faints away again.*)

PETER (*to* POPPY) She's not herself today.
  (MARY *enters from the hall and ushers in a taxi-driver carrying a large trunk with* B.P. *painted on it. He puts it down behind* ALBERT *and marches out.* MARY *follows.*)

GEORGE Mary! Marjorie! Quick, get the smelling salts!

ESTHER What she needs is a drop of water.
  (*She seizes the vase of flowers off the table, takes out the flowers and advances on* GEORGE.)

GEORGE Esther! Go away. Don't you dare!

ESTHER Here you are, dear. (*She makes ready to throw.*)

GEORGE Help!
  (*He tries to hide behind* MRS. TRUDGE *but* ESTHER *changes her mind and instead of throwing the water offers* MRS. TRUDGE *a sip.*
  ALBERT *puts on the bowler hat, sits cross-legged and starts to sing, staring blankly ahead.*)

ALBERT (*singing*) Oh dear, what can the matter be. Three old ladies locked in the——
  (PETER *puts his hand round* ALBERT's *mouth.*)

PETER Ssh! Not in front of Fred.

GEORGE (*desperate*) I can't hold on much longer. (*Calls.*) Marjorie!

FRED Here is a police message.

GEORGE Shut up!

FRED There's no need to be nasty!

(MARY *re-enters with the taxi-man. They are this time carrying a bee-hive. They advance D.L. and put it down in front of the sofa.*)

POPPY What's that?

TAXI-MAN Bee-hive.

GEORGE But I don't want a bee-hive.

TAXI-MAN Can't help that. The gentleman said to bring it up 'ere from the station. So 'ere it is. And it's full of bees. I can 'ear 'em buzzing.

ESTHER (*crossing to the bee-hive*) Bees! The little darlings. They're so good for rheumatism.

PETER Who wants rheumatism?

TAXI-MAN That'll be fifteen bob for the taxi.

(ESTHER *presents him with the flowers from the vase.*)

ESTHER Take these, my good man.

(*The taxi-man retires scratching his head, to stand by the hall door.*)

GEORGE (*calling*) Marjorie! Oh dear! (*To* MRS. TRUDGE.) Do wake up, there's a good woman. (*Calls.*) Marjorie!

(PETER *leaves* ALBERT *and goes to help.*)

PETER Here, let me help.

ALBERT (*without the restraint of* PETER'*s hand: sings*) There was a country vicarage with ivy round the wall——

(PETER *dives back and obliterates the rest.* MARJORIE *enters from the lab, trailing two long wires.*)

MARJORIE Did you call, dear?

GEORGE (*shouts*) Don't pull those wires. You'll short out the——

There is a flash and a loud bang from the cupboard. BEN *staggers out with a black face.* FRED *starts ringing like mad and his pointer whirls round and round.* ALBERT *jumps on to the sofa.* PETER *and* MARY *embrace and* PETER *loses his wig again.* ESTHER *throws the water over* GEORGE, *who drops* MRS. TRUDGE *in a heap on the floor.*

CURTAIN

ACT III

The same, after lunch that day.
The room is still in something of a turmoil, although the bee-hive and the trunk have disappeared. The table is covered with a cloth but there is nothing on it except a set of condiments. The bowler is back on the bust.

> POPPY *is discovered using the telephone. She is dressed in a white lab coat.*

POPPY (*into the telephone*) Hallo? Is that Television House?— I want Special Features—No, there's nothing wrong with the ones I've got. I want to speak to the man in charge of Special Features—Thank you—Hallo?—Oh, hallo, Michael. This is Poppy Blossom here. Listen, I'm on to something big!—No, not a new parlour game, it's even better than that. I've discovered a machine that can tell the future—— What do you mean 'is that all'! Think what we could do with it on television! We could pre-record the news for a month at a time—and —and have a programme called—er—

FRED In Town Next Year.

POPPY Yes, In Town Next Year—thanks!

FRED Not at all.

POPPY (*realising who has spoken*) Oh! (*Into phone.*) Michael, It just spoke to me!—What?—Borrow the plans? Oh, I don't know—You would? Oh Michael, would you really? I'd steal the Crown Jewels for that. Leave it to me! 'Bye now.
(*She puts down the telephone.*) A part in Coronation Street! Thanks, Fred!
(*She blows* FRED *a kiss and goes out through the french windows, calling:*)
Mr. Shaw! Oh Mr. Shaw!
(MARJORIE *and* MARY *enter from the kitchen.*)

MARJORIE What a mess! You'd think there'd been a battle in here.
MARY Well, it was a bit hectic while it lasted.
MARJORIE Poor George. He hates fuss. (*She picks up the condiment stand but drops the salt.*)
Oh dear, there goes the salt!
MARY Oh oh! Bad luck! Thank goodness auntie is still upstairs sleeping it off. She'd have us all bowing three times to the East or something.
MARJORIE (*brushing up the salt with her hands*) I hate superstitions. (*She throws salt over her left shoulder.*)
MARY Is auntie all right? (*She crosses to sofa and puts the cushions straight.*)
MARJORIE (*taking the condiments to the sideboard*) Just a thick head. It's not to be wondered at. She and Mr. Shorter seem to have polished off half a bottle of whisky before lunch. (*She holds up the empty bottle to prove it.*) Now they're both out flat.
MARY Poor Mr. Shorter. I can't help feeling sorry for him. First he loses his trousers. Now he's lost his equilibrium.
MARJORIE Well, at least Ben managed to stop him singing naughty songs.
(MARY *picks up an empty banana skin from the floor and holds it at arm's length with an expression of distaste.*)
MARY The morning after! Poor daddy, I thought he was going to go off pop. Do you think he'll ever forgive Uncle Ben?
MARJORIE (*starting to fold the tablecloth*) I don't know, I'm sure. He's so upset about his computer he doesn't seem able to think about anything else. (*Indicating the empty skin.*) Put that in the coal-bin, would you, dear? It looks like a desiccated hangover.
(MARY *walks D.L. and drops the banana into the bin which stands below the window alcove.*)
MARY Where is daddy?
FRED Mr. Shaw is in the laboratory.
MARY Oh, thanks. Did you do it much damage?
MARJORIE Evidently not. But you know what your father's like. One little blue flash and you'd think he'd been struck by lightning. (*She tucks the cloth under her arm and surveys the room.*) There now, that's a bit better.

MARY What do you think of Miss Blossom?

MARJORIE Who, dear? Oh, George's new assistant. She seems a nice
girl.

MARY You don't think she's the sort that—well—give men
ideas?

MARJORIE I hope not! No, no. She's a nice quiet girl I'd say. Not
the sort to run after a man.

(POPPY *comes rushing in at the french window.*)

POPPY Mr. Shaw! Oh Mr. Shaw! (*To* MARJORIE.) Excuse me!
(*She runs between them and up the stairs.*)

MARJORIE (*calling after her*) He's in the laboratory! These town
people—always in a hurry. What were you saying,
dear?

MARY It doesn't matter. (*She goes to look out of the window.*)
Peter's a long time.

MARJORIE He went down to the village, didn't he? To get some
electrical equipment for your father. (*She crosses* R. *of
sofa.*) Worried about him already?

MARY No, not really. (*She closes the french windows.*) Except
that he's a bit susceptible.

MARJORIE My dear girl, all men are susceptible. It's the only way
they can keep their self-respect.

MARY But——

MARJORIE Now don't worry. Peter's a nice boy and I'm sure Miss
Blossom's not up to any mischief.

FRED Psst!

MARJORIE What, dear?

MARY It wasn't me.

FRED Psst!

MARY It's Fred. He's very talkative today.

FRED She's after something.

MARY There you are! Fred knows his onions.

FRED She's planning to steal the Crown Jewels.

MARJORIE You see. He's talking through the back of his bleed-pipe.
George reckons he's suffering from amnesia.

MARY I hope you're right but I don't like the glint in that
girl's eye. Did you notice how she kept handing Peter
things at lunch?

MARJORIE Now stop imagining things. I don't suppose——
(*Someone taps at the french window.*)

What's that?

MARY (*looking out*) It's Uncle Ben.

(*She opens the window and* BEN *peers cautiously in.*)

BEN Coast clear?

MARY (*conspiratorially*) Yes, it's all right, you can come in. Daddy is in the lab.

(BEN *enters and* MARY *leaves the french window open.*)

MARJORIE Where have you been?

BEN (*below sofa*) Oh, just taking a breath of fresh air. Thought I'd let the dust settle for a bit. Is there anything to eat?

MARJORIE We've had our lunch, I'm afraid.

MARY (*on* BEN's L.) Well, some of us have anyway—bread and cheese and pickles. Mrs. T. was too upset to cook anything and Aunt Esther and Mr. Shorter were pickled already.

BEN How's George?

MARJORIE Very cross! He's taken refuge in the lab and keeps sending Peter out for bits and pieces.

MARY We think he's making you an electric chair.

MARJORIE And poor Mrs. Trudge is nursing her grievances in the kitchen.

BEN A bit sore, eh? I've got some embrocation in my trunk. (*He points to the hall and makes swigging motions with his arm.*)

MARJORIE (*moving below table*) She's noticeably tender.

MARY And she's threatening to tender her notice too.

BEN (*crossing* MARJORIE) Think it would do any good if I had a word with her? Sort of smoke a pipe of peace.

MARJORIE Well, it can't do any harm, I suppose.

MARY As long as you don't smoke your home-grown tobacco!

MARJORIE And do be diplomatic, Ben.

BEN I'll be as tactful as a tick in a tiger's tail. Leave it to me. (*He crosses to the kitchen door.*) Besides, there may be some cheese and pickles left over.

MARJORIE Ben, you're incorrigible.

BEN Hungry too!

(*He opens the kitchen door.* POPPY *comes steaming downstairs, across in front of* BEN *and* MARJORIE.)

POPPY Mr. Shaw! Oh Mr. Shaw! (*She goes out to kitchen.*)

FRED   (*calling*) He's in the laboratory!
        (*The doorbell rings.*)

MARJORIE (*to* MARY) Go and see who it is, dear, would you? Mrs.
        Trudge isn't answering the door any more today.
        (MARY *goes out to hall.*)
        (*To* BEN.) By the bye, what became of the bees?

BEN   (*pointing*) I put them under the stairs. They're a bit upset
        after the journey. I shouldn't be surprised if they
        swarmed; better keep the door shut. (*He goes out to the
        kitchen.*)

MARJORIE I must remember to warn Mrs. Trudge not to wear her
        flowery hat.
        (PETER *and* MARY *enter from the hall. He is carrying a
        paper bag and has discarded his wig and spectacles.*)

MARY   It's Peter.

PETER   Hallo, Mrs. Shaw. I'm back.

MARJORIE So I see. I must say you look better without that wig.

PETER   It's a weight off my mind. I say, do you think it'll be
        all right? I couldn't get the wire Mr. Shaw wanted.
        (*He digs in the paper bag.*) So I got some string
        instead.
        (*He comes* D.C. *displaying his purchase—a large ball of
        twine.*)

MARY   Honestly, Peter!

PETER   It's the strongest they had.

MARJORIE I'm sure he'll be delighted.

PETER   I hope so. (*Confidentially.*) I don't really know much
        about computers, you know.

MARY   You're telling us!

MARJORIE Never mind, you'll soon pick it up.

MARY   (*taking* PETER's *arm*) Peter's studying for the bar.

MARJORIE How interesting. You can show me how to make a
        Bloody Mary.

MARY   Wrong bar, dear. He's going to be a lawyer—or is it a
        solicitor?

MARJORIE So that's why he was wearing a wig! What fun! You'll
        be soliciting all over the place.

MARY   Oh no he won't! Not if he's married to me!

MARJORIE I always hoped Mary wouldn't marry one of those clever
        young men—they're such a bore.

PETER   Thanks!

MARJORIE   You know what I mean.

PETER   Where's Poppy?

MARY   Miss Blossom is taking a run round the house. I think she went into the kitchen the last time through.

PETER   I wonder if she wants a hand?

(*He goes to move towards the kitchen but* MARY *stops him.*)

MARY   You stay right here.

MARJORIE   That reminds me. Has George agreed yet? To you and Mary I mean.

PETER   Er—no. I haven't actually asked him yet. But I'm going to the very next time I see him.

MARY   Goody for you.

(GEORGE *comes bursting in from the lab looking like a thundercloud and carrying a sheaf of papers. He heads for the cupboard under the stairs.*)

GEORGE   Another fuse gone. Nothing but trouble.

MARJORIE   I shouldn't go in there, dear, the bees——

(*But it's too late.* GEORGE *is already in the cupboard. There is a howl and he re-appears, flapping about wildly with his papers. He slams the door behind him.* PETER *and* MARY *move up to help.*)

GEORGE   Ow! Go away! Help! Get off, you wretched little—— Ow! (*He slaps himself on the neck.*) I've been stung! (*He picks an imaginary bee off his neck, throws it on the floor and jumps up and down on it violently.*)

PETER   (*examining the floor closely*) I think it's dead.

GEORGE   Of course it's dead! Where's the blue bag? Marjorie, get the blue bag quick!

MARJORIE   Yes dear, all right. I think it's in the larder. (*She goes out to the kitchen.*)

GEORGE   Who the devil put bees in the cubby-hole? Next thing they'll get into the machine.

(FRED *emits a loud buzz.*)

FRED   Ouch!

GEORGE   There, you see. They'll get into everything and I shall finish up with sticky terminals. (*He puts the papers down on the table.*)

PETER   Nasty.

GEORGE (*to* MARY) Where's that uncle of yours?

MARY (D.C.) Uncle Ben? He's out in the kitchen.

GEORGE (*crossing to sofa*) Well, get him in quick. This is an emergency. (*He sinks on to the sofa, still clutching his neck.*)

MARY (*to* PETER *as she crosses to kitchen*) Go on—ask him!

PETER Hmmm?

MARY You know! (*She points to her wedding finger and goes out to kitchen.*)

PETER Oh! Yes.

GEORGE It's throbbing like a boil. Bees! If they've ruined any-thing—I'll—I'll——!
(PETER *picks up the twine and crosses to* R. *of sofa.*)

PETER Mr. Shaw?

GEORGE What the blazes do you want?

PETER I—I've got the twine.

GEORGE I'll bet it doesn't hurt like this does.

PETER No, no, the string.

GEORGE String? What's that for?

PETER I couldn't get wire.

GEORGE What the devil are you talking about?

PETER I thought it would do as well.

GEORGE I don't know what you're blathering about. Come here and make yourself useful. See if you can get the sting out.
(PETER *puts the string on the sofa and inspects* GEORGE's *neck.*)
Can you see anything?

PETER Yes. It's got a little bag on the end.

GEORGE I don't care if it's got a trunk—get it out!

FRED In 1964 ten people died of bee stings.

GEORGE I don't wish to know that!

PETER (*picking at the sting*) Hold still then. Oh, I wanted to ask you, Mr. Shaw, if I could marry——

GEORGE (*leaping to his feet with a yell*) Ow! Have you got it out?

PETER (*moving D.C., inspecting his fingers*) No—it's a hair!

GEORGE Good God man! You didn't have to scalp me!
(MARJORIE *and* POPPY *enter from the kitchen.* MARJORIE *carries a small bottle of cochineal.*)

MARJORIE The blue-bag is under the stairs with the bees. So I've brought the cochineal instead.

GEORGE About time too. I'm half bald. (*Seeing* POPPY.) Oh there you are. I've been stung.

(POPPY *crosses to* GEORGE, *pushing* PETER *aside*.)

POPPY Let me. (*She deftly removes the sting.*) There.

GEORGE You see. Never felt a thing. Thank you, my dear.

(*He glares at* PETER *who looks foolish.* GEORGE *then goes to listen at the cupboard.* MARJORIE *follows and dabs his neck with cochineal. She puts the bottle on the table by* GEORGE's *papers.*)

They're still there. I can hear them buzzing. Where's Ben?

MARJORIE I'll go and see. (*She goes out to the kitchen.*)

POPPY What happens if they go radio-active?

PETER Luminous honey.

GEORGE Dear, oh dear. (*To* PETER.) What were you saying about marrying?

PETER Oh, I was just going to ask you if I could marry— (*In his excitement he knocks over the cochineal.*)

GEORGE My blue-prints! You young idiot. Look at 'em. Covered in cochineal.

PETER Oh dear, they've turned into purple prints!

POPPY Here, let me help.

(*She seizes them and retreats* D.L. *as* BEN *enters from the kitchen. His pipe is going like a chimney and he is carrying a small pair of bellows of the type used by gardeners to puff derris dust on their roses.*)

BEN What's all this then? Have you been interfering with my bees?

GEORGE (*coming* D.C.) Interfering—! The little horrors have barricaded themselves under the stairs.

BEN They're very sensitive things, bees. You've got to treat 'em right.

GEORGE What do you expect me to do—lend them my hat to nest in? Look here!

(*He shows* BEN *his sore neck very red with cochineal.*)

BEN What's that then, sunburn?

GEORGE It is not sunburn! One of your bees stung me.

BEN Ah, they soon know if somebody don't like 'em. But

you shouldn't have let it sting you—it kills 'em, you
know. One minute buzzing about happily, the next——
(*He snaps his fingers.*)

GEORGE Well, get the little buzzers out of my cubby-hole.

BEN Right-ho! Keep your hair on. Now then—— (*He gives
his bellows a trial puff and, wreathed in smoke from his
pipe, he throws open the cupboard door and. marches
in.*) Come along, my pretties. Come along now.
(*He shuts the door behind him.* GEORGE *and* PETER
retreat D.R. POPPY *meanwhile has been edging towards
the french windows with the blue-prints clutched to her
bosom.*)

FRED Stop thief!
(POPPY *shakes her fist at* FRED *and turns it into a gay
wave to* GEORGE.)

GEORGE Dear, oh dear. (*He sees* POPPY.) Ah, you've got the plans,
I see.

POPPY (*guiltily*) Oh yes! I was just taking them to—er—have
a look in the daylight.

GEORGE Interested, eh?

POPPY Oh yes, fascinated.

GEORGE It's really very simple, you see. Basically it works on
the principle of——

PETER Mr. Shaw?

GEORGE Oh, what is it now? You're worse than the bees.

PETER May I——?

GEORGE Yes, yes. Second on the right in the hall. (*He demon-
strates the plan to* POPPY.) Here now, you start off with
the main input and——

PETER No, no, you don't understand. I want to marry——
(BEN *re-enters from the cupboard carrying a large cardboard box with a lid on it.* GEORGE *and* POPPY *retreat
rapidly D.R. below table.*)

GEORGE What's that?

BEN Bees. Lovely swarm. Worth a load of hay, this lot. Want
a look?
(*He advances towards them and they back still further
away.*)

GEORGE No. No thanks.
(BEN *trips and nearly drops the box.*)

Look out!

(GEORGE, PETER *and* POPPY *all react and get as far away from* BEN *as possible*.)

BEN They won't hurt you. You haven't got such a thing as a spare beehive, I suppose?

(GEORGE *shakes his head*.)

No. I didn't think you would have. Oh well. I'll find somewhere outside. Come along, my pretties. Let's find you a nice new home.

(*He goes out to hall with his box and the others relax*.)

GEORGE All clear, eh? (*To* POPPY.) Now come along, lass, and let me show you what makes Fred tick. Assuming he's still working.

(*He leads the way to the lab door.* POPPY *follows, still clutching the plans*.)

Oh you won't need those. Leave them out here for now.

(*Reluctantly she puts the plans on the table*.)

(*To* PETER.) Keep an eye on them, lad, they're valuable.

PETER Mr. Shaw, I want to——

GEORGE Not now, lad, not now. Work to be done.

(*He goes out to lab with* POPPY.)

PETER (*calling*) But I want to marry Mary! Oh what's the use!

(*He stands disconsolately in front of* FRED.)

What would you do, chum?

FRED Have a quick one.

PETER Good idea! (*He goes to mix a drink at the sideboard*.) I wonder why all the prettiest girls have to have such fat-headed fathers?

(*He lifts the glass to* FRED.)

Cheers!

FRED Bottoms up!

(PETER *drinks.* MARY *looks in from the kitchen*.)

MARY Did you call?

PETER No—yes—oh, I don't know.

MARY What did daddy say?

PETER He wouldn't even listen.

MARY (*crossing* L.) Oh Peter, darling. You're hopeless. You must make him listen. (*She sits on the sofa*.)

PETER But how? He's so wrapped up in his wretched machine. He thinks of nothing else.

MARY I've got an idea. Come here.
> (PETER *joins her on the sofa and she starts to whisper in his ear.*)

PETER (*giggling*) You're blowing in my ear.

MARY Don't be silly. Listen. It's a plan. (*She whispers again.*)

PETER Yes, I see. Right. Yes—yes——
> (*While they are at it* BEN *re-enters from the hall wearing a bee-keeper's hat and carrying the bellows. He stands over them above the sofa.*)
> Right ho! I'll do it. Let me just——
> (*He suddenly catches sight of* BEN.)
> Help!
> (MARY *screams.* PETER *runs behind her* D.L. *for protection.*)

BEN (*coming* D.C. *and taking off his hat*) Like it? I picked it up cheap at a Government surplus.

PETER I thought they'd got me for a minute.

BEN I only wear it for show. One good puff on the old bellows and they're on their knees. What were you two up to, if it isn't a rude answer? (*He lays the hat and bellows down on the sofa.*)

MARY We've thought of a way to make daddy change his mind about Peter and me.

BEN What are you going to do, let Esther hypnotize him?

PETER No, we'll let Fred do it.

BEN Don't tell me he can do that too!

MARY No, no. We'll make Fred change his mind. Daddy always takes his advice.

BEN (*to* PETER) But you don't know how to work it, do you?

MARY No. But I do. Or at least I know enough to get what I want.

BEN Women usually do.

PETER But we shall need your help. We've got to drag George away from the machine long enough to fix it.

BEN How about a deal? I'll help to get George out of the way if you get Fred to answer these questions. (*He takes out* ALBERT's *bit of paper.*)

PETER (*reading over his shoulder*) 'Newmarket two-thirty——' Sounds like racing.

BEN It is racing and I want the results.

MARY That's easy. Just ask him. (*She indicates* FRED.)

BEN You mean just say it aloud?

MARY Yes. You push this button and talk into here.

BEN (*going to* FRED) It sounds too easy.

MARY It is easy. You try.

PETER (*moving R. of* FRED) He answers back.

MARY (*moving L. of* FRED) Come on, Uncle Ben. Don't be shy.

BEN Right-ho!

MARY Stand on the platform.

(BEN *does so and inspects his list.*)

BEN You're not having me on, are you? I feel a right Charlie talking to a machine.

MARY No, it's all right, I promise.

(BEN *clears his throat and addresses* FRED.)

BEN (*shouting*) Now listen!

MARY You don't have to shout.

BEN Sorry! Do I have to call it—him anything?

MARY No. But press the button first.

BEN Eh? Oh yes. (*He presses the button and speaks into the machine.*) Can you forecast the following—Newmarket two-thirty, Thursday?

(FRED *buzzes and answers.*)

FRED Rice pudding!

BEN Rice pudding?

FRED Or semolina.

BEN What's that, a dead heat?

PETER It's a cold sticky mess.

BEN I've never heard of those two horses. (*To* MARY.) Are you sure he knows what he's talking about?

(ALBERT *appears and creeps shakily down the stairs and into the room. He is dressed as for Act One.*)

MARY I expect that was a menu. He throws in snacky bits like that now and again.

PETER He'll have you hanging your hat in the cupboard given half a chance. (*He sees* ALBERT.) Hello! Talk about dead heats! Look who's here.

MARY Oh, Mr. Shorter! You've found your clothes. How are you?

ALBERT (*collapsing on to the sofa*) Not well at all.

MARY We were just trying out the computer.

BEN Yes. You ought to be interested. The first race was won
by a semolina pudding! The going was a bit heavy.
(*But* ALBERT *has his head in his hands.*)
Well, let's have another go. (*To* FRED.) Now let's have
less of the *à la carte* and a bit more of the *à la* horse.
Are you sitting comfortably? Then I'll begin. Try again.
(*Loudly into the machine.*) Newmarket two-thirty!

FRED Newmarket two-thirty. Thundery showers.
(ALBERT *reacts immediately.*)

BEN (*after a pause*) Is that all?

PETER He hasn't 'warmed up yet. Try another one.

BEN (*consulting his list*) How about Goodwood three-forty-
five?

FRED Mist.

BEN Missed what?

FRED Mist—clearing later. Sunny periods.
(ALBERT *jumps to his feet.*)

BEN Oh, this is ridiculous. We're wasting our time.
(*But* ALBERT *has come to life and steps forward with
his eyes shining with excitement.*)

ALBERT (*up C.*) No, no. Go on. It's wonderful!

MARY But all we get is weather forecasts.

ALBERT Yes, it's amazing. Try another one. (*He shouts over
BEN's shoulder.*) What about Kempton Park four
o'clock?

FRED Wet and windy!

BEN Serves you right for shouting.

PETER Was that a forecast or another menu?

ALBERT (*clapping his hands and skipping D.C. in glee*) Oh! Isn't
it exciting?

BEN (*moving down above table*) Absolutely ripping!

MARY (*moving above sofa*) Sorry, Uncle Ben, Fred is usually
better than that. It must be the bees.

ALBERT But why be sorry? It's perfect—perfect. He gets it right
every time. Oh this is most exciting!
(*The telephone rings and* PETER *answers.*)

BEN (*R. of* ALBERT) You mean that's what you wanted?

ALBERT Yes, of course.

PETER (*into telephone*) Hallo?—Who?—Oh yes. He's here.
(*To* ALBERT.) It's for you.

ALBERT   Me?

PETER   Yes, it's the Met. Office.

ALBERT   (*hurrying to the phone*) Excuse me. (*Into telephone.*) Shorter reporting.

    (PETER *joins* MARY *above sofa.* BEN *sits* L. *of table.*)

BEN   Short of brains if you ask me.

ALBERT   (*into phone*) Oh yes, sir. Good morning, sir—I mean good afternoon.—Yes, sir, absolutely true, sir. Yes, yes, right every time.—Quite, quite. Incredible—but true I assure you—That's very good of you, sir. I do my little best.—Yes, sir, I'll negotiate at once. Goodbye, sir. (*He puts the phone down and turns to the others triumphantly.*) That was the Chief Forecaster.

PETER   From the Met. Office?

ALBERT   Yes.

BEN   Old Cumulo-nimbus himself?

MARY   You mean to say you're a Met. man?

ALBERT   Yes. I'm in charge of Mist and Drizzle.

PETER   I've never met a Met. man.

BEN   Well, you have now. No wonder our met is so wet.

MARY   But why are you so interested in Fred?

ALBERT   (D.C.) My dear young lady. You've no idea what it's like. For years we've been doing our best. Up early in the morning watering the seaweed, feeding the shepherds, blowing up balloons. And what do we get? Snoots and higgers!

PETER   What?

ALBERT   I mean hoots and sniggers. And never enough money to make both ends met. Even the roof leaks. I can't stand it any more. (*He almost sobs.*)

MARY   There, there.

ALBERT   We get threatening letters too. Last week a man from Manchester offered to come up and starch my cold front.

BEN   Awful!

ALBERT   So you see, when we heard of a machine that could really forecast the future we had to find out if it was true.

PETER   And is it?

ALBERT   Yes! Three questions about weather conditions at Newmarket and Goodwood next week and it was right every time!

BEN But how do you know it was right?

ALBERT Because it's precisely the opposite of what we forecast, so it must be right. Think of it—right every time! No more apologising to the mayor of Weston-super-Mare and hiding from the neighbours. I've got to have that machine! (*He seizes* PETER *by the lapels and shakes him.*) You've got to let me have it!

PETER Help!

(BEN *and* MARY *lift* ALBERT *off and soothe him down.*)

BEN Now, now. Simmer down!

MARY There, there. Come and sit down.

(*She leads* ALBERT *to the sofa, where he sits. She stands L. of sofa.* PETER *crosses above table, smoothing his suit back into place.*)

PETER Hit him over the head with an isobar or something!

ALBERT I—I'm sorry. I was carried away.

BEN You will be if you go on like that.

PETER (*picking up the plans*) I wonder how it works?

BEN What have you got there?

PETER Hmmm? Oh these are the plans.

ALBERT (*rising*) The plans of the computer!

(*He crosses between* PETER *and* BEN *and grabs the plans.* MARY *crosses to L. of* BEN.)

BEN Oh no you don't! (*He grabs them from* ALBERT.)

MARY Thank you!

(*She grabs the plans from* BEN *and throws them to* PETER *who catches them. Suddenly* GEORGE *enters from the lab and crosses to the hall. They stand motionless and follow him with their eyes. He walks slower and slower and, at the door, turns uneasily and finds them all looking at him.*)

GEORGE I'm—just—er—just—going outside.

FRED Second on the right.

(GEORGE *goes out. At once bedlam breaks out again.* ALBERT *grabs the plans and runs round the room with them with* PETER *and* BEN *in hot pursuit.* MARY *plucks the plans out of his hand as he runs past and pops them into* PETER's *hands.*)

MARY   I think you had better look after these.

PETER   Why me?

MARY   (*whispering*) Because we want to fix the computer, remember?

PETER   (*also in a whisper*) Oh, I see.

MARY   (*to* BEN) Well, we kept our part of the bargain.

BEN   What? Oh yes. You want me to keep George amused for a bit. Tell you what. (*He hands* ALBERT *across to* MARY.) You take old Deep Depression here for a walk to cool him off and I'll attend to George.

MARY   (*taking* ALBERT'*s hand*) Come on, Mr. Shorter. A bit of fresh air will do us all good.

ALBERT But I don't like fresh air. I want to talk to Mr. Shaw.

BEN   (*pushing him towards the window*) Don't you be a naughty meteorolololologist or I'll give you a thump on the barometer. Off you go.

MARY   Come along and you can tell me all about your nice anticyclones.
        (*She propels a reluctant* ALBERT *through the french windows.* BEN *stops* PETER *as he goes past.*)

BEN   I shouldn't take the plans. They might get wet.

PETER   What? Oh yes.
        (*He hands the plans to* BEN *and goes out through french window.*)

BEN   (*calling after them*) And don't hurry back! (*He crosses to C. tapping the plans thoughtfully and stands looking at* FRED. *Then he picks up his bellows off the sofa and peers up the spout.*) This works like a charm on the bees; it ought to keep old George quiet.
        (GEORGE *shouts, off, and dashes in from the hall.*)

GEORGE The bees! Somebody's put 'em in the loo.
        (BEN *dusts him down liberally with his bellows.*)
        What on earth are you do——?
        (*He freezes rigid.* BEN *puts down the bellows.*)

BEN   There now. That'll put pollen on your pistil! (*He gets behind* GEORGE *and steers him stiffly towards the cupboard.*) Into the cubby-hole. Oh, half a tick. (BEN *leaves* GEORGE *like a wax-work by the cupboard door and goes to get the bee-hat off the sofa. Slowly* GEORGE *begins to topple over.* BEN *rushes back and catches him just in time. He props him upright but as soon as he turns away to pick up the hat* GEORGE *begins to sway again.* BEN *just manages to grab the hat and get back to prevent his total collapse. He pops the hat and veil over* GEORGE's *head.*)

There we are now. You look lovely. In we go.

(*He pushes* GEORGE *into the cupboard and shuts the door and locks it. He dusts his hands in satisfaction.*)

Now then! (*He takes a crumpled newspaper from his pocket.*) Let's have a basinful of modern science.

(*He steps up to* FRED *and starts to manipulate the knobs, reading from the paper.*)

Racing at Kempton Park today. Now what about the winner of the three-thirty?

FRED   The Galloping Major.

BEN   Lovely! Goodwood two-forty-five?

(ALBERT *re-enters through the french window.*)

FRED   Sailor Sam.

ALBERT   What are you doing?

BEN   (*hastening to him*) Ah! it's old Wet and Windy. (*He hustles him to the stairs.*) Just the chap I was looking for. I've got something to show you upstairs.

ALBERT   I don't want to go up there. I might meet Esther.

BEN   Nonsense, my little old mate. You just come along with me.

(*They go up the stairs.* BEN *takes the plans with him. As they disappear* PETER *and* MARY *enter through the french window.*)

PETER   Nobody about.

MARY   Good. Now's our chance. Bring the plans.

(*She goes into the lab.*)

PETER   Plans, plans.

(*He looks on the table, then under it.*)

MARY   (*off*) Hurry up, darling. Have you found them?

(PETER *tries to stand up and bangs his head on the table.*)

PETER   Blast!

MARY   (*off*) What, darling?

PETER   No. I haven't found them yet.

(*He scrambles out and lifts the bowler off the bust and looks underneath.*)

Excuse me!

(MARY *enters from the lab.*)

MARY Well, they're not in there. Oh, do hurry up and find them, Peter. Daddy will be back any minute.

PETER I can't understand it. I left them here on the table when we went out—I think. They've just disappeared.

MARY (*looking under the cushions on the sofa*) Oh damn! Trust a man to lose something at a critical moment.

PETER (*coming to C.*) Can't you fix the machine without them?

MARY Not a chance. It's much too complicated. You don't think Mr. Shorter took them? I knew we shouldn't have let him come back on his own!

PETER He said he felt a forecast coming on.

MARY Where is he, by the way?

PETER I don't know. I haven't seen him.

MARY (*crossing below table*) Have you tried under the sofa?

PETER He won't be under there. It's too low.

(*During this dialogue* BEN *creeps down the stairs with the plans and tiptoes across to the kitchen door where he goes out unobserved.*)

MARY Fool! I meant the plans.

PETER Oh! (*He looks.*) No. Only bits of fluff.

MARY Well, they must be somewhere.

PETER Do you think we ought to try Aunt Esther's room?

MARY No, better not. I expect she's still sleeping it off. And she's always warning daddy to keep his hands off her paraphernalia.

PETER Yes, quite!

MARY Perhaps mummy has tidied up in here.

PETER (*looking round*) It doesn't look much like it.

MARY It never does. I'll go and ask if she's seen them. You try in the sideboard.

(MARY *goes out to the kitchen.* PETER *crosses to the sideboard and starts to forage in the bottom cupboard.* POPPY *enters from the lab. She has taken off her spectacles and loosened her hair which flows abundantly over her shoulders. The lab coat has gone and she looks very seductive in a tight blouse and short skirt. She comes to stand behind* PETER *who is busy disinterring papers and books from the sideboard cupboard, mutter-*

ing to himself as he throws them over his shoulder.)

PETER (*reading the titles*) 'Mind and the Machine'; 'Spherical Trigonometry'; 'Calculus'; 'Winnie the Pooh'; 'Lady Chatterley's Lover'. (*He almost throws this too but stops short and begins to turn the pages with interest.*)

POPPY Looking for something?

PETER (*throwing the book up in the air*) Wazzat?
(*He turns to find himself face to knee-cap with* POPPY. *Slowly he straightens up, enjoying the scenery en route.*) Oh it's you, Miss Bosom—Blossom. I didn't recognise you down there. It is you, isn't it?

POPPY You can call me Poppy.
(*He backs away C.,* POPPY *following.*)

PETER Oh good. I used to press flowers. I—er—I was just having a tidy up.

POPPY Looking for a hiding-place, Peter?

PETER No—that's to say—well——
(*He backs D.L. as she comes closer.*)

POPPY Let's look together, shall we?

PETER Well, I don't know. Mary wouldn't—I mean I wouldn't —oops!
(*He falls over the arm of the sofa and lies like a beetle on its back.* POPPY *sits beside him and leans perilously close.*)

POPPY Two are better than one!

PETER (*with his nose flattened against her chest*) You can say that again!

POPPY Two heads.

PETER (*disappointed*) Oh!

POPPY Peter's got something Poppy wants.

PETER Good grief! Have I?

POPPY (*crossly*) Oh come on. Don't play cat and mouse with me. You've got the plans, haven't you?

PETER Well, I did have before we went out.

POPPY (*stroking his head*) And it's such a responsibility! Poor boy, why don't you let me look after them for you?

PETER But I haven't—I haven't!

POPPY Just a weeny peep, that's all I want. You'd find me ever so grateful! (*She leans closer still, showing a great deal of shapely leg in the process.*)

PETER   Yes, I dare say. But you see, the fact is——
> (MARY *enters from the kitchen on this interesting tableau.*)

MARY   Mummy says she hasn't seen—oh Peter!
> (POPPY *springs up and goes* D.L. PETER *struggles to a sitting position.*)

PETER   Hallo darling! Miss Blossom was just trying to get a weeny peep.

MARY   So I see! I suppose you found her under the sofa with the other bits of fluff!

PETER   (*standing*) No, actually I was looking in the sideboard.

MARY   I don't want to hear, thank you. I believe you've lost those plans deliberately. (*She sits disconsolately* R. *of table.*)

POPPY   Lost them?

PETER   Yes, I was trying to tell you. When we came back they'd disappeared.
> (ESTHER *appears on the staircase behind* PETER. *She is a trifle pale but as regal as ever.*)

POPPY   That's odd because Mr. Shaw has vanished too.

ESTHER   (*loudly*) Vanished! Ooh! (*She clutches her head.*)

PETER   (*jumping violently*) Oh my hat! (*He backs up* R.)

ESTHER   Oh my head!

PETER   Well, if it isn't Nellie Dean. How's the hangover?

ESTHER   (*coming* D.C.) I shall complain to the grocer about that last bottle of fruit juice. It was definitely not up to standard. Now what's all this about George disappearing?

POPPY   He's just disappeared and he seems to have taken the plans with him.

ESTHER   (*thoughtfully*) Yes, he's just about the right age.

MARY   The right age for what?

ESTHER   Why, for kicking over the traces with some young— (*She looks hard at* POPPY.) Where have I seen you before?

PETER   I think it was near the old mill by the stream.

ESTHER   What?

PETER   (*crossing* R. *of* ESTHER) Never mind. This is Miss Blossom. She's here to help Mr. Shaw.

ESTHER   To help him to do what?

PETER   And I'm Peter Puller.

ESTHER   Oh yes, I remember you. You're going to marry Mary.

MARY (*looking up with red eyes*) That's what he thinks.

PETER (*going to her*) But Mary darling!

MARY (*turning her back*) Don't you talk to me you—you philanthropist you!

PETER Philanderer.

MARY (*facing him again*) Oh, you admit it, do you?

ESTHER I didn't know you collected stamps, Peter. Remind me to show you my post-marks some time.

PETER That'll be fun.

POPPY Never mind about post-marks. What about finding the blue-prints?

ESTHER Oh yes, the ones George is supposed to have taken with him. (*She wanders* D.L.) Well, I suppose I could try my crystal ball, but it's not terribly reliable this time of the year.

PETER Sun spots?

ESTHER No, condensation actually. I've got it!

PETER I was afraid you had.

ESTHER (*rubbing her hands in triumph*) We'll ask Humphrey.

PETER Who's Humphrey—the curate?

ESTHER Good gracious no! Humphrey is my contact on the other side.

POPPY The other side of what?

MARY Oh no! you don't mean——

ESTHER (*to* C.) Yes, yes, that's it. We'll have a séance. It's a splendid opportunity. I haven't had a séance since I charmed the warts off the butcher's boy.

PETER Did it work?

ESTHER Oh yes! Of course. He gets boils now.

MARY (*coming forward*) Auntie dear, do you think we should? Remember last time? All that sticky stuff on the dining table?

POPPY (*awestruck*) Ectoplasm?

MARY No, custard. We knocked it over in the dark.

PETER Talking about that, isn't this an odd time of day for a séance? I thought ghosts only walked after dark.

ESTHER Superstitious nonsense! Now come along. (*She moves* U.C. *and claps her hands.*) Get the chairs round the table and close the curtains. Peter, put on the side-light, it will give us atmosphere.

(PETER *turns on the standard lamp and brings down the chair from* U.L. MARY *meanwhile fetches the chair from* U.R. *and* POPPY *draws the curtains.*)

PETER That's all we needed! A matinée performance. We shan't be able to hear ourselves speak for the rattling of teacups. (*In sepulchral tones.*) Can you tell spook from butter? (*Behind* POPPY.) Whoooo!

POPPY (*jumping*) I wish you wouldn't do that!

ESTHER Where's Marjorie? She must make up the number.

MARY Mummy's in the kitchen, but don't you think——

ESTHER (*at the kitchen door*) Marjorie!
(MARY *shrugs and sits in one of the chairs.*)
We won't ask Mrs. Trudge. She isn't quite the type.

POPPY (L. *of table*) I've never been to a séance before.

PETER And I've never been swimming on Christmas Day but that's no reason to start now.

MARY (*to* PETER) I don't see what you're grumbling about. Soft lights should just about suit you.

ESTHER What about Mr. Shorter?

PETER He certainly doesn't suit me!

POPPY I believe he's upstairs. I don't think we ought to disturb him.

ESTHER No, perhaps not. I'm not altogether happy about that young man. Come along, sit down. Peter over here. Miss—er—um——

POPPY Blossom.

ESTHER Yes, that's right. You sit over there and Marjorie can be there. (*She indicates the chair below the table.*)
(MARJORIE *enters from the kitchen with an apron.*)
Ah! There you are.

MARJORIE It's a bit early for Canasta, isn't it?

PETER It's not cards, Mrs. Shaw. We're going to raise a ghost.

ESTHER Not a ghost, dear, a friend from the other side.

MARJORIE Oh dear, and I'm wearing my old apron.

ESTHER Humphrey won't mind. He's very broad-minded about things like that. Now come along, dear, we need you to make up the circle.

MARJORIE But I'm icing a cake.

ESTHER Never mind that. There are more things in heaven and earth than jam sponge.

PETER   Fish and chips for instance.

MARJORIE   But this is a birthday cake for George. Oh all right, just
           for a minute. But I mustn't be long. It's taken me since
           lunch to persuade Mrs. Trudge not to give her notice.
           (*She sits down between* MARY *and* POPPY. *The order is*
           MARY *on extreme R.,* PETER *on her L., then* ESTHER,
           POPPY *and* MARJORIE.)

ESTHER   (*sitting down*) First class. Now, all hold hands.

MARY   I am not holding his hand and that's flat.

PETER   If only you would let me explain.

ESTHER   Now stop bickering, you two.

POPPY   I don't mind holding his hand. It makes me feel safe.
           (PETER *goes to move his chair round to* POPPY'*s side of
           the table but* MARY *grabs him.*)

MARY   Here, give it to me!
           (*They all hold hands.*)

ESTHER   Now, are we ready? All quiet. Concentrate. Concen-
           trate. Is there a spirit in the room?
           (*The voice of* MRS. TRUDGE *is raised in song in the
           kitchen.*)

MRS. TRUDGE (*off*) I'm in the mood for love,
                Simply because you're near me!

ESTHER   (*at the top of her voice*) Mrs. Trudge! Belt up!

PETER   I should think that's frightened off every ghost between
           here and Leighton Buzzard.

MARJORIE   Oh dear, I do hope she's not upset.

PETER   What about me? I've gone deaf in one ear.

MARY   Ssh!

ESTHER   Is there a spirit in the room? One knock for yes, two
           knocks for no.

PETER   How the devil can it give two knocks if it isn't there?

POPPY   Ssh!

ESTHER   (*moaning*) Oh! Oh! Oh!

MARJORIE   Whatever's the matter?

PETER   It's the fruit-juice coming on again.

ESTHER   Be quiet. I'm trying to tune in.

PETER   I think you've got Channel Two.

ESTHER   Ssh! Something's going to happen.

PETER   Oh goody!

FRED   Lighting-up time today is at seven-thirty.

PETER   Good old Fred.

FRED   Eskimos are taller than pygmies, especially when sitting down.

ESTHER Oh do turn it off, someone!

FRED   In cold climates, extremities tend to be shorter.

PETER   (*turning him off*) Bad luck!

ESTHER Now perhaps we can get on. Oh spirits, we have a boon to ask. One knock for yes, two knocks for no.
(*Nothing happens.*)
Somebody else have a go.

PETER   We have a bone to pick with you. Knock us up when you're gliding through.
(*There are two distinct knocks from the cupboard under the stairs.*)
Good lord!

POPPY   Oh! I'm frightened!

ESTHER Ssh! It's a presence.

PETER   No, it isn't. It's an absence. It gave two knocks.

MARY   Peter, be quiet.

ESTHER Is that you, Humphrey?
(*Confused knocking and moaning.*)

PETER   He's been at the fruit juice too.

ESTHER Are you happy?
(*More moans.*)

PETER   He sounds hilarious.

ESTHER Ssh! Something is going to happen. I can feel a manifestation coming on.

PETER   It's probably wind. What on earth!
(*Because there is a scuffling round the bend of the stairs and an odd figure in white appears and comes hopping into the centre of the room. It appears at first sight to be a pudding cloth with legs but is in fact* ALBERT SHORTER *imprisoned in* GEORGE's *combinations. These have been tied over the top of his head with string. His arms are inside. During the preceding scene the lights can be slowly dimmed leaving the group at the table in an eerie greenish pool of light.* ALBERT, *when he appears, can also be spot-lighted in green.*
The séance jumps to its feet and scatters. POPPY *and* MARY *scream and cling on to* PETER *who picks up the*

bust to defend his honour. ESTHER *clasps her hands in ecstasy.*)

MARY ⎫
POPPY ⎬ (*together*) ⎧ Peter!
MARJORIE ⎭ ⎨ Oh!
⎩ Good heavens!

ESTHER   Wonderful. Wonderful!

(MRS. TRUDGE *enters from the kitchen bearing. an iced cake with candles.*)

MRS. TRUDGE   'Ere we are then. That's finished. Do you want me to put it in the—— (*She comes face to missing face with the apparition.*) Oh my Gawd! It's the 'eadless 'orseman! (*She drops the cake with a plop and scampers off back to her kitchen as fast as her game leg will let her.*)

MARJORIE   Oh dear! She's upset again. (*To* ALBERT) Do excuse me. (*She goes chasing after* MRS. TRUDGE *into the kitchen, calling.*) Don't worry, Mrs Trudge, it's only a ghost!

(ESTHER *comes to* ALBERT'*s* L. *and gingerly prods him.*)

ESTHER   Yes, quite substantial. A materialisation at last!

MARY   (*crossing to* C.) Yes, and I recognise the material. I'd know those combinations anywhere. Daddy, come on out of there. (*She starts to untie the string at the top. The lighting returns to normal.*) And stop fooling around!

(*Out comes* ALBERT'*s head complete with gag, his eyes bulging.*)

ALBERT   Mmmm! Mmmm!

ESTHER ⎫ (*together*) ⎧ Mr. Shorter!
PETER ⎭ ⎨ Albert!

MARY   Oh, it's you.

ALBERT   Mmmmm! Mmmmm! (*He hops up and down wagging his head.*)

ESTHER   (*glaring into* ALBERT'*s face*) How dare you interfere with my manifestation! You've ruined everything. Just as it was all going so well. I shall go to my room and cast a horoscope. Out of my way!

(ALBERT *hops smartly* L. *and* ESTHER *sweeps past but turns on the stairs to deliver a parting broadside.*)

And I hope Humphrey haunts you!

MARY   Poor auntie. She is upset! (*Crossing to* ALBERT.) But how did he get in this state? Is it some sort of experiment, do you think?

PETER Could be.

ALBERT Hmmm! Mmmm! Grrr! Mmp!

PETER (*below table*) He's trying to say something.

ALBERT Grrmp! Mump! (*He jumps up and down violently.*)

POPPY (*to C.*) I wonder what he wants? Do you think we ought to let him out?
(ALBERT *nods emphatically.*)

PETER I suppose so.
(MARY *unties the gag and* ALBERT *emerges spluttering.*)

MARY There we are. That's better. What happened?

ALBERT Oh, that dreadful man!

PETER George?

ALBERT No the other one, with the flashy suit.

PETER Uncle Ben!

ALBERT Yes. He tied me up. He's run off with the plans.

MARY So that's where they've gone. Here, sit down and have a rest.
(ALBERT *hops over and collapses on to sofa L., still half-clad in the combinations.*)

POPPY (*anxiously moving above sofa*) Are you sure he took the plans with him?

ALBERT I think he did. But I could only see out through the—er—armhole.

PETER Have a drink.

ALBERT No thanks!
(*They are interrupted by more knocking from the cupboard.*)

POPPY Listen!
(*More knocking.*)
It's Humphrey. He's still here! (*She backs away to a safer position D.L.*)

PETER And what's more he's in the cupboard! (*He strides up to the cupboard.*)

MARY (*backing below table*) Oh Peter, be careful.
(PETER *flings open the door and reveals* GEORGE *still in his bee-hat.*)

PETER Well I never! He's got his head in a meat-safe.
(PETER *lifts it off and* GEORGE *blinks in the light.*)

MARY } (together) { Daddy!
POPPY }   { Mr. Shaw!

GEORGE Where is he?

MARY Who?

GEORGE That—that uncle of yours! It's all his fault. He's a menace to civilised society. I'll run him out of the house.

PETER It sounds as if he's already run.

MARY Come and sit down, daddy.

(*She and* POPPY *lead* GEORGE *down to the sofa.*)

GEORGE I don't want to sit down! I just want to lay my hands on him!

(*They plonk him down next to* ALBERT, *who smiles at him nervously.*)

He dusted me down with derris and stuffed me in the cubby hole. Grrr!

POPPY (*stroking his forehead*) Poor Mr. Shaw!

MARY (*surveying the couple on the sofa*) Uncle Ben seems to have left quite a trail.

PETER (*putting the bee-hat on the table*) Yes. They make a handsome pair, don't they?

POPPY (*to* MR. SHAW) Never mind. We'll take care of you.

(GEORGE *pats* POPPY's *hand.*)

GEORGE Thank you, my dear. I'm glad somebody cares.

ALBERT What about me?

GEORGE Well, don't just sit there like the man who didn't take Eno's. Go and find him.

ALBERT Who, me?

PETER I don't think it'll do much good. He must be miles away by now.

ALBERT Not if there's a betting shop near, he isn't.

GEORGE There's one in the village.

ALBERT Then that's where he is.

MARY But why?

ALBERT He said Fred had given him all the winners for this afternoon's races and he was going off to make his fortune.

GEORGE Serve him right then.

PETER How's that?

GEORGE Because he'll lose every penny.

MARY (*to sofa*) But daddy. You said Fred never makes a mistake.

GEORGE I know, my dear, but I was wrong. I've discovered a serious fault in his ungulator.

POPPY But the plans——

GEORGE Oh there's nothing wrong with the plans. It's the wiring that's wrong. I seem to have coupled up the transformer to the——

MARY But daddy, if Fred isn't perfect—you mean I don't have to marry a red-haired man after all?

GEORGE No, I'm afraid not, my dear. Not unless you want to of course.

MARY (*moving above table to* PETER) Oh Peter, darling!

PETER Darling!

(*They go into a long kiss and remain oblivious to everything else that happens until the final curtain comes down.*)

GEORGE No, she doesn't want to. Oh well!

POPPY (*coming D.R. of sofa*) But what about Uncle Ben?

(*This is the cue for* BEN *to enter through the french windows in a great rage. He crosses above sofa and shakes his fist at* FRED.)

BEN Ten bob each way on every race and I lost my shirt. Call that thing a computer!

(GEORGE *and* ALBERT *have both jumped to their feet and they point accusingly at* BEN.)

GEORGE ⎫
ALBERT ⎬ (*together*) That's him!

BEN (*realising the situation*) Well, I think I'll be off.

(*He turns and runs out through the hall door.* GEORGE *pushes* POPPY *aside and chases U.C. after him with angry shouts.*)

GEORGE Come back here. Just you wait until I lay my hands on you. I'll stuff your head in your beehive.

(*He goes out through the hall door.*)

ALBERT Stop thief!

(*He makes to follow them but falls flat on his face because his feet get tangled in his combinations.*)

Help!

(POPPY *goes to help him but before she can do much*

BEN *bursts in again through the french windows,
followed by* GEORGE. FRED *starts to play* 'Post Horn
Gallop' *loud and clear as they leap over* ALBERT *who
ducks just in time, leap over the remnants of the cake
and dash out into the kitchen.*)

BEN (*as he clears* ALBERT) Heads down. Clicketty-click.
Sorry, I forgot my hat.
(*He picks the bee-hat off the table as he passes and goes
out to the kitchen.*)

GEORGE (*passing through*) Come back here you—— Excuse me!
(*As he jumps over* ALBERT.) You thieving no-good son
of a flat-capped, horse-loving bee-keeper!
(*He goes out to kitchen and* FRED's *tune falls to a
murmur.* ALBERT *sits up and* MARY *and* PETER, *still embracing, ease down to R. of sofa.* BEN *and* GEORGE *re-
appear immediately from the kitchen.* FRED *bursts into
full blast.* ALBERT *ducks and they leap over him and
disappear out of the french window.*)

BEN (*jumping* ALBERT) Hup and over! (*He goes out.*)

GEORGE Don't you think you can get away from—— Mind your
head—me! Come back here, you two-timing, double-
dealing tobacco-grower! (*He goes out.*)
(FRED's *music sinks to a gentle background.* MARJORIE
comes in from the kitchen holding the plans.)

MARJORIE (*calling*) Oh George! George dear! I wonder if this is
what they were looking for. (*She waves the plans.*) I
found them behind the fridge.

POPPY ⎫
ALBERT ⎬ (*together*) The plans!
(POPPY *lets* ALBERT's *head fall on to the floor with a
thump, rushes over and grabs the plans from* MARJORIE.
ALBERT *scrambles to his feet and hops across arms outstretched.* PETER *and* MARY *sink on to the sofa still
embracing.*)

POPPY Yes, it's them!

ALBERT No, they're mine!
(POPPY *eludes him and runs upstairs with the plans.*
ALBERT *tries to untangle his legs and hop upstairs after
her at the same time.*)
They're mine. I must have them or they'll run me out

of Mist and Drizzle and demote me to Fost and Frog. I must have them, I must! Miss Blossom! (*And he stumbles out of sight up the stairs.*)

MARJORIE (*easing towards* C.) Well, really I don't know what's come into everybody today, do you, Mary? (*She takes in what* PETER *and* MARY *are doing.*) Oh well, at least they're not getting into any mischief. Now where did I put that knitting? Ah there it is. (MARJORIE *picks up her knitting from the sideboard and sits* L. *of table and starts to knit.*) That's a pretty tune, Fred.

At once FRED *bursts into full blast with the* Post Horn Gallop. BEN *and* GEORGE *come legging across from the french window.* BEN *makes a noise like a huntsman's horn and* GEORGE *cries 'Yoicks. Yoicks! Tallyho!' as they thunder across. They jump over the missing* ALBERT *and out into the kitchen.* MARJORIE *nods benevolently at them as they pass by and continues placidly with her knitting.*

As they disappear into the kitchen POPPY *and* ALBERT *come running down the stairs, pursued by* ESTHER *wielding a besom broom. They all three gallop across at a great lick and out into the kitchen.*

No sooner in than everyone re-appears—BEN (*wearing his bee-hat*); GEORGE (*waving a screw-driver*); POPPY (*brandishing the plans*); ALBERT (*still in his combinations*); ESTHER (*now astride her broom*)—*and last, but not least,* MRS. TRUDGE (*brandishing a large frying pan*). *In time to the 'Post Horn Gallop' they run like a chorus line across the stage, all in step and lifting their knees high. In front of* MARJORIE *who nods approvingly and carries on knitting, in front of* PETER *and* MARY *lost in their marathon embrace and out through the french window.*

CURTAIN

PRODUCTION NOTE

This is a play about Fred—a computer with a heart of gold and a mind of his own! To judge by the number of visitors, young and old, who spend happy hours pressing buttons and pulling levers at the Science Museum, machines hold a special fascination for us all. And the more nearly human they are the more we seem to like them. So it should be with Fred. After the surprise of his first intervention it should be possible to establish an atmosphere of sympathy and collusion between Fred and the audience so that we feel an almost proprietary delight in his unexpected and yet somehow inevitable commentaries on the antics of the other players.

As always with farce, timing and pace are all-important. The dialogue should bubble along like a mountain stream, sweeping the audience from one unlikely situation to the next and avoiding backwaters like the plague.

Peter, Mary and Marjorie are relatively uncomplicated characters; the rest exhibit various degrees of eccentricity. Mary is a modern miss, pretty and vivacious with a stubborn streak, determined to get her man though all the wonders of modern science may stand in the way. Peter is a cheerful and well-meaning young fellow but not too bright and rather out of his depth in this unconventional household. Both these parts need a light touch and all the enthusiasm of youth.

Years of marriage to George have inured Marjorie to the unexpected and she remains unperturbed amidst family crises, strange visitations and things that go bang in the night. Perhaps, mercifully, a little withdrawn from reality (if the events at 26 Walnut Grove can be said to bear any resemblance to reality), she is a contented soul and still young enough herself to be fully on the side of youth.

With George we begin to cross the border into the bizarre, although he would be the last to notice it. He is not so much absent-minded as single-minded. He knows every knob and wire in Fred's innards by heart but probably hasn't noticed the colour of his wife's eyes for years. However, he should not be made to appear too unworldly and remote and can be allowed a certain gleeful satisfaction from his one diversion—provoking Esther.

Esther is, in many ways, the opposite of George and yet, at the same time, shares his singleness of mind. For her science stopped short at Nostradamus and it is all written in the stars. An opportunity here for some strong character acting. Everything about Esther should be larger than life. Costume, voice and gesture should all combine to suggest a man o' war, all sails set, billowing down on its unsuspecting victims.

Chief victim is Albert Shorter, the errant Met. man. Humourless and dedicated, he is the inevitable target for Esther's attentions and any other odd arrows of misfortune that happen to be flying around. His whole appearance should be as doleful as drizzle on a summer day and only in Act Three when he declares his real identity can he be allowed a fleeting moment of dignity before his final undoing.

Uncle Ben is a rascally old extrovert with so engaging a personality that we can forgive even his fondness for practical jokes. A flashy appearance and abundant energy will help to put this character across.

Poppy Blossom and Mrs. Trudge complete the main cast. Poppy conceals her true colours behind a delicious façade. A seductive young woman, her figure-work in both senses of the word should appear beyond reproach. Mrs. Trudge's charms, on the other hand, are somewhat past their prime and the years have left her cantankerous and highly suspicious, as well she might be, of the various goings-on which interfere with her household chores.

And so to Fred. Unlike many of his more malicious contemporaries, Fred is an agreeable fellow—a friend of the family not averse to joining in the conversation when occasion demands. The Shaws treat him as an established fact of life. Only the unsuspecting visitors should show any surprise at his various irreverent and inconsequential asides. And here a word of warning may be in order. Fred's conversation must not be obscured in a welter of 'atmospherics'. The aim must be to convey the idea of a mechanical voice without too much distortion. This is not as alarming as it may sound. If a society happens to number an electronics expert among its members, well and good; let him have his head with flashing lights, oscilloscopes, echo chambers etc. But with limited resources a satisfactory Fred can be achieved with a painted scenery flat and a loud-speaker, or even a well-placed actor with a suitable edge to his voice. Whatever method is adopted, however, it is clearly important to test for sound before the actual performance.

Fred apart, staging and lighting are straightforward although, as suggested in the script, special lighting may be used to excellent effect during the séance scene in Act Three. The 'explosion' at the end of Act Two should preferably be fired electrically to ensure precise timing and the accompanying smoke can be produced in a number of ways but probably the best results are achieved by placing 'smoke powder' on a sheet of mica over an electric heater.

Finally—for safety's sake—two points of detail. The use of a plastic bottle will avoid unacceptable damage to Mrs. Trudge in Act Two while Albert should be allowed an adequate spy-hole in his outsize combinations in Act Three to enable him to hop downstairs without colliding with the scenery or breaking his neck.

J.A.D.

FURNITURE AND PROPERTY PLOT

ACT I

ON STAGE

Sofa (L.C.)
 On it
 Cushions
 Magazine
  Library book

Standard lamp (U.L.)

Sideboard (U.R.)
 On it
 A bottle of whisky (opened)
 A plastic bottle of fruit juice
  (half empty)
 Glasses
 A plaster bust (sex indeter-
  minate)
 Telephone
 The insides of an old clock
 Transistor radio
 Ornaments

 In the drawer
 A large pack needle on thread

 In sideboard cupboard
 Books (inc. 'Lady Chatterley's
  Lover')
 Newspapers
 Magazines

Small dining table (R.C.)
 On it
 Magazines
 Local newspaper
 Vase of flowers

Five dining chairs (three by the
 table, one by the standard lamp
 and one above the sideboard)

Carpets and rugs

French window curtains (closed)
 and pelmet

Cushions

Waste-paper bin (D.L.)

OFFSTAGE

 In kitchen
 Fire tongs (MRS. TRUDGE)
 Beads (MRS. TRUDGE)
 Two cups of tea on tray (one
  glued to saucer with no liquid
  inside) (MARJORIE)

 In cupboard under stairs
 Hats (inc. large bowler)
 Bundle of wires

PERSONAL

Penny (PETER)
Spectacles (MARJORIE)
Small screwdriver (GEORGE)
Duster (MRS. TRUDGE)
Small suitcase (POPPY)

ACT II

STRIKE

Teacups and tray
Newspaper
Small suitcase

CURTAINS OPEN

SET

 On sideboard
 Pot of tea
 Milk jug
 Sugar basin
 Four cups and saucers
 Packet of cornflakes

 On table
 Cloth
 'The Times'
 Woman's magazine
 'Chick's Own' comic
 Four cereal plates, knives, forks
 and spoons
 Toast-rack with toast

Marmalade jar
Butter dish
Bowl of fruit with apples and bananas
Vase of flowers (a little water in the bottom)
Four napkins
Almanac

On sofa
White lab coat
Magazine

OFFSTAGE

In kitchen
Tray with kipper on plate (MAR-JORIE)
Lavatory brush and cleaner (MRS. TRUDGE)

Upstairs
Pair of socks in parcel (MARY)
Large book (ESTHER)
Chest expander (ALBERT)
Empty bottle for spare drink (ESTHER)

In laboratory
Large screwdriver (GEORGE)
Lengths of wire (MARJORIE)

Off L.
Parcel with long-johns and letter (MARJORIE)
Birthday cards (MARJORIE)
Large trunk ⎫ (TAXI-DRIVER)
Beehive   ⎭

PERSONAL

ALBERT Notebook and pencil
Wallet with pound notes
List of questions
BEN Pipe and matches
POPPY Handbag
Newspaper cutting
Certificates
PETER Handkerchief
Wig
Spectacles without lenses

ACT III

STRIKE

Crockery from sideboard
Breakfast things from table except condiments
Trunk and bee-hive
Parcels and cards

SET

On sideboard
Knitting
Bowler back on bust

CHECK

Banana skin on floor

OFFSTAGE

In kitchen
Bottle of cochineal (MARJORIE)
Cotton wool (MARJORIE)
Small gardener's bellows (BEN)
Iced cake (MRS. TRUDGE)
Duplicate plans of computer (MARJORIE)
Large screwdriver (GEORGE)
Frying pan (MRS. TRUDGE)

Upstairs
Combinations and gag (ALBERT)
Besom broom (ESTHER)

In laboratory
Plans of computer (GEORGE)

Cupboard under stairs
Cardboard box for bees (BEN)

Off L.
Paper carrier bag with ball of string (PETER)
Bee-keeper's veiled hat (BEN)

PERSONAL

List of questions (BEN)
Newspaper (BEN)
Apron (MARJORIE)

MADE AND PRINTED IN GREAT BRITAIN BY
LATIMER TREND & COMPANY LTD PLYMOUTH

MADE IN ENGLAND